This volume has been produced in response to requests from readers of *The Naxos Mysteries*. Greek food plays a notable part in the books, and reading them has awakened an appetite for cooking it at home.

A Greek Feast on Naxos contains more than recipes. There is a short 'foodie' story in the *Naxos Mysteries* series, called A Greek Feast on Naxos. There are also articles covering some of the iconic foods of the Cyclades, suggestions for finding ingredients outside Greece, recommendations for other sources of Greek recipes, and a culinary route to follow round the south coast of Naxos when you next visit the island, following the trail of the characters in the books.

The Naxos Mysteries combine archaeology and crime in the idyllic setting of the Cyclades. The main character, Martin Day, is an eccentric archaeologist with a passion for the ancient history of Greece and a hatred of antiquity crime. According to the police, his approach is one of guesswork, intuition and risk. According to his friends, it is exciting but exasperating. Above all, Day is a lover of Greek cuisine.

Vanessa Gordon lives in Surrey, studied English and Irish literature, and spent her career in the music industry. She loves Greek food at least as much as Martin Day.

BY THE SAME AUTHOR

The Naxos Mysteries

The Meaning of Friday

The Search for Artemis

Black Acorns

The Disappearance of Ophelia Blue

The Reach of the Past

A Greek Feast On Naxos

An Outpouring of Affection for Greek Cuisine

Vanessa Gordon

Published by Pomeg Books 2023

Copyright 'A Greek Feast on Naxos': Vanessa Gordon 2023

Particular recipe copyrights: Aglaia Kremezi (Tou Yiaourtiou; Koulourakia Methismena), Yiannis Vassilas (Eggplant Caviar; Beetroot Salad; Fennel Fritters; Axiotissa Stuffed Vegetables), Eat Yourself Greek (Kalogeros), The Friends of Paros and Antiparos (Pitarakia)

Photography copyright: Vanessa & Alan Gordon (all images except Kitron); Yiota Vouzna (Kitron image)

All rights reserved. No part of this publication may be reproduced, stored in a retrieval system, or transmitted in any form or by any means, electronic, mechanical, photocopy, recording or otherwise, without prior written permission of the copyright owner. Nor can it be circulated in any form of binding or cover other than that in which it is published and without similar condition including this condition being imposed on a subsequent purchaser.

ISBN 978-1-7393053-3-8

This book uses both imperial and metric measurements. Follow the same units of measurement throughout; do not mix metric and imperial. Cooking times given are a guide only, and will differ according to ingredients and ovens.

Pomeg Books is an imprint of
Dolman Scott Ltd
www.dolmanscott.co.uk

We should look for someone to eat and drink with before looking for something to eat and drink.

Epicurus (341-270 BCE)

CONTENTS

	PAGE
Preface	viii
The Naxos Mysteries and Greek Food	1
A GREEK FEAST ON NAXOS A Foodie Story	2-22
List of Recipes	24
About the Chefs	25
THE RECIPES	26-52
The Food Paradise of Naxos	54
Famous Naxian Cheeses	55
Mastic, Turpentine and Pistachio	56
Kitron - The Liqueur of Naxos	57
Gouna - Sun-Dried Mackerel	58
Capers and Chickpeas	59
Oregano, Sweet Pelargonium and other Herbs	60
Honey	61
Foodie Excerpts from *The Naxos Mysteries*	64
A Drive round Naxos	76
Online Suppliers in the UK	77
Suggestions for Further Reading on Greek Food & Wine	78
Some Greek Explained	79
Index of Recipes	80

PREFACE

A Greek Feast on Naxos has been created especially for the readers of *The Naxos Mysteries* who have enjoyed the food in the series almost as much as the mysteries themselves.

Some people have told me that they would like to recreate Greek cuisine at home, where home is beyond the borders of Greece; this little volume is the result. I hope the recipes and suggestions here prove a useful starting point, and that you enjoy many wonderful home-cooked Greek dinners in future. Do remember that (as my husband would say) I am an expert in *eating* Greek food rather than in *cooking* it, which is why I am very grateful for the enthusiasm and support of several really good cooks. I also hope you will enjoy this book for its own sake, as a bit of fun.

I have made a few suggestions for further reading, and for online suppliers of foods and ingredients in the UK, as well as listing the sources of the recipes in this book where you will find many more.

You will notice the variety of weights and measures that appear in the recipes, for which I apologise, but they are as written by the cooks themselves, whose words I don't want to change.

I have also included some little extras for you, including snippets about the food and drink of Naxos, food-related excerpts from the books, and a little tour of Naxos which you can try out when you visit. It includes places to stop and eat!

The new short story, *A Greek Feast on Naxos*, fits into the series after *The Reach of the Past*. (Readers may like to turn to the back of the book to confirm the meaning of the occasional Greek words and phrases in italics.) The story is meant to be light and celebrate the Greek cuisine that I love, but in it you will recognise characters from the *Mysteries* and at least one little outstanding uncertainty will be resolved for you. This is a little present for the readers who have asked me for the answer.

Vanessa

THE NAXOS MYSTERIES and GREEK FOOD

Throughout the series, from the very first of Martin Day's adventures (*The Meaning of Friday*), meals have been of great importance both to Day and to his friends. Rarely does he himself cook, and when he does his enthusiasm exceeds his expertise. My goodness, though, how he enjoys his food. He is especially fond of eating at his local taverna, Taverna O Thanasis, asking the cook Koula for her daily recommendations. His preference is to order several dishes to share, accompanied by red wine 'from the barrel'; this is the local wine which has never seen a bottle. He wouldn't thank you for sweet food, and he doesn't care for olives, but crispy little lamb chops, delicious chips, roasted potatoes, and salad dressed with fine Greek olive oil: these things restore his faith in life. Not that he has ever lost it since buying his house on Naxos.

Naxos is an island with outstanding food. The cheeses are superb and made locally; indeed, some are unique to the island. The potatoes have great flavour and texture, and the vegetables are fresh and sun-ripened. As Day's author, nothing could prevent me from making him adore Greek cuisine, and so the books contain quite a lot of it. I began to hear from readers that they would like me to give them a few recipes. I'm more of an expert eater of Greek food than a cook, but here are some tasty ideas with additional suggestions for ingredients available outside Greece.

This small volume has taken a long time to prepare, unlike the dishes on the following pages. The short story that follows forms part of *The Naxos Mysteries* and takes place some months after the end of *The Reach of the Past*. If you have enjoyed the earlier books you will, I hope, enjoy being reunited with some of the characters you met in them. You could even play a silly game of 'which book did he/she come from?' However, if this is your first encounter with Martin Day, I hope you might be tempted to explore Day's earlier adventures, when you're not too busy in the kitchen.

This is not the end of *The Naxos Mysteries*. Not by any means. It is the beginning of a new and even more exciting period of Day's life. He has come of age; it took him until he was forty. He has Helen, he has learned many lessons, and nothing will stop him from seizing life with both hands. That can only mean that we have more of his impetuous, inspired and intuitive escapades still to enjoy.

A GREEK FEAST ON NAXOS
A Foodie Story for readers of *The Naxos Mysteries*

Archaeologist and TV presenter Martin Day was using the internet to remind himself how to tie a Windsor knot.

He rarely needed to wear a tie in Greece, and had thrown away his meagre collection when he left England. He had bought this one a few weeks ago for their wedding in London. It was the brightest thing in his wardrobe by a considerable margin, and he liked that. The colour symbolised the start of a different period of his life.

'Don't tell me you're still struggling with that!' chuckled Helen, finding him squinting at the screen, tie dangling from his hand.

He straightened up and stared at her, uncharacteristically lost for words. How could he not have noticed that dress in their luggage, or seen it in the house since they arrived back on Naxos? The delicate embroidery on the shoulders was its only decoration, but it needed nothing more. The dusty blue colour reminded him of a warm Greek sky at dawn.

'You look beautiful!' he said, shaking his head with a grin.

She turned her back to him and lifted her hair, wanting his help with her necklace. He fastened the clasp and kissed her neck.

'Forget the tie, darling. You don't really like them, do you?'

'It's okay, I'm not going to be beaten. There! Is that all right?'

'It's fine. It looks good. You don't often wear bright colours.'

Before he could tell her how the colours matched his current mood, there was a knock at the front door.

'Ah, that will be Orestis with the car,' he said instead. 'Are we ready to go?'

They closed the windows and shutters against the heat, and left the cool of the house for the bright sunshine of the road. Orestis and his old Mercedes were right outside. Orestis grinned and opened the back door with ceremony. From the porch of the neighbouring house, Stavros and Soula called out good wishes. There were few secrets in the village of Filoti.

They were finally on the way to their wedding reception. It was not being held in a London hotel, nor directly after their ceremony, but weeks later, in the hills of Naxos. The venue was a place called Taverna Agnanti. The name Agnanti was an unusual one, carrying the idea of having a bird's-eye view. It was a fine name for this restaurant, whose terrace overlooked the surrounding hills and the spreading plain, all the way to the coast and the distant waters of the Aegean.

A Celebration of Cuisine in the Cyclades from the author of The Naxos Mysteries

Thirty guests had accepted their invitation, including many who lived outside Greece. Day had not expected people to jump at the chance to come all the way to the Cyclades simply for a party, but that is what happened. Some were going to make a holiday of it, and had booked accommodation on the island. He had given some accommodation at the Elias House, which he ran as a kind of guest house for artists. Nobody was staying with them in Filoti, though; tonight they wanted to be alone together.

Orestis drove sedately from Filoti to Apeiranthos and then on to the Taverna Agnanti. He showed unusual restraint on the winding road through the foothills of the island's central peaks, as he felt befitted the occasion. Orestis wore several hats in addition to his current rôle as their driver: he was an experienced restorer of historic buildings and the business partner of their friend Nick Kiloziglou. He was also the brother of one of the owners of the Agnanti. Naxos was a small island that way.

They soon drew up at the Agnanti. A rambling stone building flanked by an unpaved car park, it was not initially impressive. On the inland side of the road, where the ground was higher, an old windmill with a broken sail stood testimony to the rural past of Naxos and the prevalent Meltemi wind. Apart from the windmill and the taverna, there was nothing for miles around except goats, and it was a long way to the nearest village. Even so, everyone on Naxos knew this restaurant. Its magic was hidden beyond its roadside façade, revealed only when you saw the dining terrace and tasted the food. As he opened the car door for Helen, Day felt a surge of the wonderful zest for life that the Greeks call *kefi*, an empowering combination of joy, optimism and good spirits.

Dimitris Diamantis was waiting for them at the door. He stood straight and tall, proud of the business he had built up, and with good reason. He and his brother-in-law, Orestis's brother Markos, owned the Taverna Agnanti, and his wife Anna ruled the kitchen. People said she was the heart of the enterprise.

'Welcome!' said Dimitris, shaking hands. 'Follow me to the terrace, please; your guests are already here, enjoying a drink. This way.'

He led the way through the cool taverna and out again into the sunshine. The terrace was full of people talking and drinking. A sturdy wooden pergola shaded the dining area, and a marble serving table was laden with glasses and baskets of bread, but not even the majestic orange bougainvillea, its flowers glowing from pale amber to luscious gold, could detract attention for long from the famous view across the slopes and cultivated plains of fertile Naxos.

Dimitris raised his voice and announced their arrival in Greek, calling them the bride and groom. Day smiled, feeling a bit too old to be called a bridegroom in any language, but he accepted a glass of Villa Amalia from a young man with a tray, and began to greet their guests.

Suzanne was Helen's oldest friend, but Day had not yet met her. When they were introduced, he discovered that she looked rather like Helen in the way that old friends sometimes do. There was a confidence and a warmth in Suzanne that he immediately liked, and as he knew that she had recently lost her husband he also found it admirable. When he offered his condolences she hesitated only fractionally before giving him a hug. He felt as if he had passed a little test. They had barely begun the overdue conversation to which he had been looking forward, when they were joined by Fabrizio Mirano.

Fabrizio embraced him and slapped him on the back, as he always did. Then he turned to Helen and Suzanne.

'Signora Day, my warmest congratulations! I'm Fabrizio. We met in London, but it was a long time ago. I'm sure you don't remember.'

'Of course I remember. This is my friend, Suzanne. Fabrizio is a colleague and friend of Martin's, a fellow archaeologist.'

'It's such a pleasure to be here!' said the Italian. 'I was sorry not to see you again when I came briefly to Naxos last year.'

So many more introductions were made in the pleasing mêlée of the next hour or so that the time passed very quickly. Lizzie and Siobhan, the vivacious librarians from the British School at Athens, were especially keen to meet Helen, having assumed for many years that Day was a confirmed bachelor. He found himself, as a result, making small talk with their husbands, while overhearing one or two anecdotes about his younger self being exchanged behind him.

The party soon began to be something of a blur to him. He made his way round the terrace, trying to speak to as many people as possible, and feeling the impossibility of doing it well.

One or two people made a particular impression on him. There was Tasos Cristopoulos, the retired Chief of Police of Naxos, who presented his wife Melina with the graceful formality typical of him. He wore the comfortable old jacket that Day remembered, the one that made him look more like an academic than a policeman. Day noted with approval that his wife carried herself with the same unassuming competence as her husband, and experienced a stab of nostalgia for the time when Cristopoulos had directed the island's police force.

In a rare moment of stillness, when he could take a drink from his glass and survey the terrace, he noticed that several people were making new connections. In particular, Peppino Berducci, the sculptor from Sicily, had identified Fabrizio as a fellow Italian and they were now deep in conversation. His close friend Andreas Nomikos had recognised Angelika Spetzou, and had introduced her to his partner, Fotini; both the women were artists, and had plenty to say to each other.

His attention was quickly distracted.

'Oh, it's Jacques, over there!'

Jacques Avian, a well-dressed man with an intelligent and slightly quizzical expression, had raised his glass in salute from across the terrace. An art historian from the Sorbonne, with a surprising knowledge of the underground trade in antiquities, Jacques had been a friend of Day's for many years.

'Jacques! Great to see you! This is Helen. Helen, this is Jacques Avian from Paris.'

'*Enchanté*, Madame!' said the Frenchman, smiling. 'I've been looking forward to meeting you.'

Day heard a note of curiosity in his friend's voice. Jacques, too, had probably assumed he was a bachelor for life.

'This is Marie-Claude,' continued Jacques, introducing his partner. 'We teach together at the Sorbonne. *Chérie*, Martin and I were together at university, a long time ago.' He lowered his voice. '*Il est un homme passionné…*'

'Mmm!' murmured Marie-Claude with a mischievous wink towards Helen.

'Passionate about antiquity, of course!' chuckled Jacques.

'How long are you going to be on Naxos?' laughed Helen. 'We must see you before you leave, if there's time. Perhaps for a meal?'

'That would be our pleasure,' said Jacques. 'We are staying for a week.'

They made a loose arrangement and chatted for a while before Jacques and Marie-Claude moved away to join another group. They were immediately joined by Day's professional colleagues from London, Maurice and Scott.

Maurice Atkinson, Day's long-suffering agent, already knew Helen. After greeting her he moved straight on to the subject closest to his heart: the series that Day would be filming during the coming months. The contract had been signed at Christmas, and Maurice was eager to get moving with it. It was up to Scott Macfarlane, the film director with whom Day usually worked, to reassure him.

'Martin is very well-organised and hard-working,' he said. 'It will be a tremendous success, Maurice. We'll be working flat out throughout the summer.'

Helen warmed to Scott and understood why Day liked him. She understood Maurice's concerns, even though today was not the time to voice them. Day's approach to life was erratic, as his agent knew very well. He had flashes of real brilliance, periods of procrastination, and fundamentally was averse to hard work unless he created it for himself.

'And I'm looking forward to it, Scott,' he said. 'Now, you should both meet Fabrizio Mirano.'

So saying, he beckoned Fabrizio over and made the introductions. Fabrizio's rôle in the forthcoming series would be an important one. He left them deep in conversation and drew Helen aside to where they could not be overheard.

'Who's that man over there by the wall, darling? I don't think I know him him. Do you? Could he be with Suzanne?'

'I was wondering that myself, a few minutes ago. No idea. I thought he must be one of your friends. Suzanne didn't say she was bringing anyone. Could he have come with Maria, maybe?'

Maria Ioannides, one of the few single women at the party, had had the least distance to travel; her family owned the Villa Myrsini on Naxos. She was chatting with a group which included Efi from the Epigraphic Museum in Athens, and did not seem to be connected to their unrecognised guest.

There was no time to ask the man himself. Dimitris was about to make another announcement.

'*Kyries kai Kyrioi*, if you would take your seats, the meal is about to be served.'

Having set things in motion, he came over to Day and Helen, led them to their table and pulled the chair out for Helen. It was this gesture that made Day realise that their hosts at the Agnanti might be enjoying the occasion almost as much as he was himself.

The tables beneath the pergola were decorated with sprigs of olive branch and red oleander flowers; baskets of bread and bottles of chilled white wine were already on each one.

Aristos Iraklidis, the Curator of the Naxos Archaeological Museum, and his wife Rania, came to sit next to them. When everyone had settled, Aristos stood up and cleared his throat. Day picked up his wine glass in the expectation of a speech.

'Good afternoon to you all, I'm Aristos Iraklidis. I'd like to mark this very special occasion with a few words. I'll be as brief as possible!'

A chuckle passed round the tables, and one person offered a quiet 'Bravo!'

'Helen and Martin have some very good friends, which should not, of course, surprise us. Everyone here has made a considerable effort to be with them today. There are those among us who have travelled from England, from France, from Italy, and from across Greece. Each of us, in another way, has made our own journey of friendship with Helen and Martin. Let me tell you a little about mine.

'I first met Martin when he moved to Athens fifteen years ago. The young colleague soon became a friend, one who was always interesting and exciting company. In the early days he was a restless character full of energy who felt pulled in various directions, but all that he did was driven by his genuine passion for the ancient history of Greece. I remember, when Martin first came to live on Naxos, he told us that he would be living here "until something else came up". I believe those were your words, Martin? In those days, he was a man with no particular plan, no ambitions, and an enviably relaxed view of life.

'That relaxed view of life hasn't changed a great deal, but something else has. A few years ago he brought Helen to meet us. They'd known each other as friends for a long time in England, and she came to Naxos for a holiday. She hoped it would be easy to write here, and we wondered whether Martin might appear in one of her novels. However, he led such an uneventful life that this seemed unlikely. Ah yes, you're clearly ahead of me. We were so wrong. Martin's life on Naxos has been anything but uneventful.'

The old man chuckled and a murmur of agreement passed round the tables.

'Martin is a changed man today,' continued the Curator, 'and we don't have to look far for the reason. He also now has a plan, he tells me. That is, he and Helen have a plan. She is, if she will allow me to say so, as clever and clear-sighted as she is beautiful. We are looking forward to seeing a great deal more of Mr and Mrs Day, this year and for years to come.

'Will you join me, please, in a traditional toast? To Martin and Helen. In Greece we say to the married couple: *Na zisete!*'

It was the traditional toast to long life and happiness. The words rippled round the tables. As she smiled her thanks to them all, Helen thought she saw the unknown guest raise his glass specifically to her.

Day stood up. It was his turn to reply, and he could do nothing about the silly grin that had spread across his face.

'Thank you very much, Aristo, and thank you, everyone.'

He allowed a small pause to hang in the air.

'*My wife and I ...*'

There were cheers and groans from the tables where their English friends were sitting. The phrase had evoked just the response he had hoped for.

'Thank you! Seriously, Helen and I are overwhelmed that so many people came here to be with us today. We hope to see many of you during your stay, but you're welcome always to visit us in our Naxos home as our guests.

'I'd like to thank our hosts, Dimitri, Anna and Marko, for making this an occasion which we'll never forget. I think I speak for everybody when I say how much we're looking forward to the feast they've prepared for us. We may not be on a beach like the young couples, but there will be dancing later, the party will go on into the night, and in our opinion this is one of the best venues on the island.'

The enthusiastic agreement took a few moments to subside.

'Tonight is about our life in Greece. When we planned this celebration, we tried to combine the things that we love about Greece with what we love about England; this reflects our life choices and the future we plan together. England is our original home, where we spent our youth, and our roots are there. Greece is important to both of us; it has worked its magic on us over the years, and this is where we will stay. I hope that by the end of your visit to Naxos, wherever your own roots lie, the beauty of Greece will have begun to captivate your hearts as it has ours.

'Speaking of beauty, Helen and I have been close friends for many years. One day, not very long ago, I realised how much more she really meant to me. Perhaps I'd spent too much time in antiquity and not enough in the world around me. I have some good friends to thank for opening my eyes to what, at one point, I was very close to losing, but it was Helen herself who helped me to see clearly. I will thank her for the rest of my life.

'So now, in the absence of a "best man", may I propose another toast, one which comes from the heart.'

He was surprised to hear a catch in his voice.

'Would you please stand and raise your glass to my precious wife, Helen!'

'To Helen!'

'Helen!'

A Celebration of Cuisine in the Cyclades from the author of The Naxos Mysteries

'La Belle Hélène!'

It was the voice of Thanasis. It was what he had always called her.

Their Greek wedding feast was about to begin.

First came the *orektika*, the small plates of freshly-prepared dips, salads and other delicious things to taste and share. This was one of Day's favourite ways of eating in Greece: picking this and that, passing and sharing plates, the perfect way to prepare the mind and appetite for the main dish to follow.

Markos, Dimitris and the staff swept round the terrace placing food on the tables within reach of every guest. There was *fava*, the yellow split pea dip topped by slivers of onion and a light swirl of olive oil. There were dishes containing creamy *melitzanosalata*, made from aubergines. The traditional Greek salad, with fresh tomato, crisp cucumber and black olives, was topped with the local Naxian cheese, Xinomyzithra, a handful of capers and a light, local dressing of vinegar and oil.

The volume of voices noticeably increased as more and more dishes arrived.

In the next wave came *tyropitakia*, small triangular pies of crisp filo pastry with a moist cheese centre, served warm from the oven; it was impossible not to pick one up in your fingers. Traditional meatballs came next, their savoury aroma drawing murmurs of approval. There were freshly-fried courgette balls, crisp on the outside and soft within, and dishes of cool, dill-covered *tzatziki*. The final plates to arrive contained tomato balls, a speciality of Santorini and one of Day's favourites.

'*Kali orexi!*' boomed Dimitris. 'Good appetite! Buon appetito!'

Offering and sharing the dishes, comparing and recommending the different foods, was all it took to break down any remaining barriers between the diners. Day watched with pleasure. Thanasis and his family, owners of the taverna in Filoti which had become his favourite regular place to eat, were discussing Greek cuisine with their neighbours and fellow taverna-owners, Vasilios and Maroula. Less predictable friendships were being made elsewhere: a rather flirtatious conversation, indeed, was now taking place between Maria and Fabrizio.

He decided that now was the moment to remove his tie and undo the top button of his shirt. He tore some crusty bread from the fresh chunk in the basket, and took some aubergine dip and some *fava* onto his plate. The delicate pieces of raw onion which were strewn on the *fava* could not be called a garnish: they were an intrinsic part of the dish. They released their mild flavour into his mouth as he crunched them, a perfect foil for the smooth, earthy split peas and the fresh, clean flavour of the bread. He could not help taking three or four more mouthfuls before being able to try anything else.

The contrast between the *fava* and the aubergine dip was very pleasing. The roasted aubergines had a depth and smokey warmth that was both rich and light, and the cook had got the texture completely right: it was neither too smooth nor too chunky. He scooped up a little more with his bread and, after eating it slowly, wiped his plate clean with the rest of the crust.

'This is very good,' he heard the Curator murmur. Aristos was savouring a little meatball, halved and dipped into *tzatziki*. The portion remaining on his plate looked moist and tempting, pieces of fresh herb visible among the meat.

Day nodded. What should he try next?

He took a little cheese pie and bit into it. The pastry was thin and crisp, and the filling still warm, soft and tangy. Was it made from sheep's or goat's milk? he wondered, but it was not important. All that mattered was that he really wanted more. He ate the rest of the little pastry and took another; it would have been wrong not to do so.

'Try the tomato balls, Martin,' said Efi from opposite him. 'They're amazing.'

He certainly had no objection to doing as she suggested. In Greek cuisine any vegetable, apparently, could be turned easily and cheaply into tasty little fritters, and even herbs were sometimes used, with a bread or potato base, to create mouth-watering delicacies. The tomato ones, however, were always particularly succulent. He took a couple from the dish, and two of the courgette balls, and opened a courgette ball first; perhaps it is in childhood that we learn to leave the best till last. The courgettes released their gentle aroma of the garden as soon as his knife had parted the crunchy exterior.

When he came to eat the tomato balls he had to acknowledge that Efi was right. They were slightly warm, and the outside gave way with a pleasing resistance to reveal the soft interior, which combined the juiciness of tomato with the aromatic excitement of Greek basil. Smaller-leaved than Italian basil, the leaves of the Greek plant are slightly sweeter, he had heard. When warm, like in these tomato balls, it epitomised the flavour of summer in the Greek islands.

'*Kalo kalokairi*,' he murmured, almost to himself. 'Here's to a good summer!'

He limited himself to a single meatball, as he wanted to save his appetite for what was still to come: the roast lamb. He dipped the meatball in the creamy, dill-infused *tzatziki*, and a combination of mint from the meatball and dill from the *tzatziki* filled his mouth, even as his tastebuds tingled to the soft beef filling.

He took a pause from the *orektika* to pour Helen and himself more water from the chilled bottle nearest to him, and in his mind he raised a glass of something special to Anna, the creator of the meal.

'I'm impressed!' smiled Rania, whose cooking Day regarded as among the best on Naxos. 'Excellent *orektika*. This *melitzanosalata* is exactly how we prefer it. So many people use mayonnaise in it these days - such a shame. The old ways are the best, don't you think?'

He agreed, and passed her the bottle of water, obeying her almost imperceptible request.

'Just a little salad for me now, I think,' he said. 'The best is yet to come. Can I pour you some wine, Rania?'

Having added a little more to her glass and chatted for a while, he turned back to the food. From the salad he picked out some succulent chunks of dark red tomato and pale cucumber, and added a generous helping of the moist cheese from the top, followed by as many of the capers as he reasonably could. Tearing off a little more bread, he soaked up the vinegary juices of the salad dressing and pushed some of the soft white cheese onto his fork, topping it with a caper.

'Mmm, the taste of summer,' he murmured to Helen, who was smiling at him over the rim of her glass. 'To taste this cheese and at the same time to smell the meat on the spit … Heaven!'

A baby began to cry, and her mother carried her into the taverna, waving to them as she passed. On her way back she stopped and bent to kiss them.

'*Na sas xaireste*!' she said

It was a traditional wish of health and happiness.

'Thank you, Deppi, and hello, little Alexandra! She's been very good today.'

'She's a good baby,' laughed Deppi, shifting the baby onto the other hip. 'This is a wonderful restaurant, it certainly deserves its reputation. Good traditional food, well cooked, everything is delicious.' She inclined her head towards where she had been sitting. 'You know we're sitting with Ben? He told us you're the nearest thing he has to a brother, Martin. Why didn't you tell us about him before?'

'We grew up together until I went to university,' Day answered, avoiding her question.

'Yes, he told us. He says he's been to Naxos before. We must all get together next time he comes. Bring him to see us in Plaka. Nick can do one of his Aussie barbecues.'

Day watched her go feeling slightly guilty. He had been captivated by her once, even though she was married to his closest friend on Naxos. There had been a kind of sad pleasure in knowing that she was completely beyond his reach. That was before he had seen the light, understood his own feelings better.

He watched Deppi reach her table and pass the baby girl to Nick. That was when Ben and he exchanged glances. Ben gave a discreet thumbs-up, his lips pressed in a tight smile. Day nodded back. It was all they needed to understand each other. Ben was coming to see them the following evening, and then they would have plenty of time to talk.

The removal of the empty dishes signalled the end of the *orektika*, and there was a sense of pleasurable expectation. The lamb, which had been turning on the spit of a large grill against the rear wall of the taverna, had been taken into the kitchen to rest, so that the juices could be reabsorbed and the meat become even more succulent.

A Greek speciality, especially at Easter, lamb had been the obvious choice for a Greek wedding celebration. Day smiled at Rania, thinking that her roasted lamb was as good as any he had ever tasted; he rarely turned down a chance to enjoy it. She tilted her head slightly and smiled at him, unaware of his current preoccupation with her cooking.

The lamb, however, was not the next thing to claim everyone's attention.

A man in his late forties, the Mycenaean expert at the British Museum, stood up with uncharacteristic shyness. At his side, his wife encouraged him.

'Hello,' he began, 'I'm Alex Harding-Jones, and this is my wife, Kate. This isn't our first visit to Naxos to see Helen and Martin, and I'm sure it won't be the last. I know I speak for us all when I say, these are very special people. Kate and I had the honour of witnessing their marriage ceremony in London a few weeks ago. It was a beautiful occasion, understated and intimate. Today here we are, enjoying a very different kind of event, full of people and laughter, and it seems there will be dancing too.

'Martin and Helen are both successful professionals: writers and public speakers. Also, as Kate and I have seen at first hand, they have some experience of unravelling the mysteries of the human heart. Small wonder, then, that Helen's novels are so well-received, and Martin has made some memorable contributions to both archaeology and police investigations.'

He raised his glass amid the murmurs of agreement. Day noticed a wry smile on the face of Chief Inspector Andreas Nomikos.

'The future will surely hold many more occasions when Helen and Martin impress us with their skill, and their abundant human kindness. We wish them every happiness!'

The short speech was well-received and Alex sat down amid applause. Day smiled his thanks. He had not expected the overt expressions of friendship, nor the compliments, and found them slightly overwhelming. He rather hoped that the red wine would soon appear, as he felt rather in need of it.

As if reading his thoughts, Markos and Dimitris brought shining jugs of red barrel wine from the kitchen and began putting them on the tables. Markos placed one in front of Day and Helen with a flourish.

'*Oriste!*' he said, and then lowered his voice slightly. 'Your violinist is happy to play now. *Endaxi?*'

'Violinist?' said Helen. 'What violinist?'

'At the far table,' said Markos, surprised, indicating the man neither of them recognised. He was holding a violin case. Day looked at Helen, who shrugged.

'Go ahead,' he said.

Markos nodded to the man, who took his instrument from its case, crossed to the wall of the terrace, and stood tuning it in the sun. People began to fall quiet. When he had finished tuning, aware that he had everyone's attention, the musician raised the violin to his shoulder.

'Mesopelaga,' he said directly to Helen. It seemed to be the name of the piece they were about to hear.

The music began. Dreamy and ethereal, the notes drifted upwards into the warm air, the melody winding itself round, both wistful and affirming. It sounded Greek but also modern, and in the musician's hands the violin became almost like a voice. Not even the children interrupted. Efi Charalambou, opposite them, was holding her hand over her mouth and moving gently with the music.

At the end of the piece the violinist sat down to enthusiastic applause. Efi turned happily back to Day and Helen.

'That was a song by Andriana Babali,' she told them. 'The words are beautiful. *In the middle of the sea, love found me while I laughed. I wasn't asking for anything, love turned me upside down.* Who's the violinist? He's wonderful.'

Luckily they were saved from having to answer. Dimitris and Markos were bringing the roast lamb from the taverna kitchen. Naxian potatoes roasted in olive oil, lemon juice and herbs surrounded the sliced meat. Everyone helped to make space between the unfinished bowls of salad and baskets of bread, the glasses and bottles and jugs of barrel wine. Dimitris sent back to the kitchen for more *tzatziki*, just as Anna herself arrived with an enormous tray of *yemista*: huge tomatoes and ripe red peppers stuffed with a filling of rice, sultanas, herbs and pine nuts. The tops of the vegetables were darkened and crisped in the oven. She placed the *yemista* on the serving table and invited everyone to help themselves.

Day sat back. He poured a little red wine into both Helen's glass and his own, and sipped contentedly. He wanted to remember this moment. The terrace was a hub of festivity in a beautiful, silent landscape. Without the taverna, there would be little to hear at this isolated location. The occasional bleat of a goat, perhaps, or the buzzing of a bee, or the quiet twittering of an invisible bird, would have been the only sounds.

The light was beginning to soften now, the afternoon to draw out; the colour of the distant sea was changing to silver, and the further peaks were losing definition.

He felt deeply happy.

He watched the violinist for a few moments, and their eyes met before the musician was drawn back into the conversation round his table. Day would have loved to know how he was explaining his presence at the party, but he was not about to ask. The lure of the fragrant roast meat and the crispy roast potatoes had just won him over.

Nobody who knew him would be surprised to learn that the first thing he tasted was a piece of roast potato. Day's love of fried potatoes was an open secret among his friends, but the roasted version came a close second, and these were very good indeed. He could detect a slight fragrance of lemon as he bit into one. A light drizzle of olive oil had been added to the dish when it came out of the oven, together with a sprinkling of fresh oregano. The result, for Day, was a small personal heaven.

And then the lamb. He laughed to himself as he remembered phrases like 'in his gut', 'at a visceral level' and 'in the pit of his stomach'. So many food metaphors had been invented for moments like these, when the smell and taste of food sparks off a powerful feeling. He was looking forward to the future more than ever before. He lifted his glass and allowed the young red wine to warm his palate and calm his momentary frisson. Helen's hand touched his; perhaps she had felt something of what he had felt, or maybe she had, as usual, simply noticed the change in him.

When justice had been done to all the food, and the plates and dishes had been cleared away, most people stood up to mingle on the terrace. Day and Helen went to stand by a young olive tree that had grown through a gap in the floor tiles near the parapet wall. Hints of pink and orange had begun to infuse the sky in the west.

'Happy?' he asked her, noticing how the sun fell on the side of her face.

'Very,' she said. 'Isn't this the best place in the world?'

She may have meant the Agnanti, or Naxos, or Greece itself. They stood enjoying the gentle light, looking out towards the placid sea and talking quietly. The party would continue into the night, there would be dancing, darkness would fall, and the scent of the sun-baked grasses on the hillsides would overtake the delicious smells of the feast.

A quiet voice behind them broke into their conversation; it was Raj Chaminda. Raj had become a close friend after the disappearance of his mother, Ophelia, two years before on Naxos. He hugged Helen affectionately and shook Day's hand.

'Congratulations!' he said. 'I'm really sorry I can't stay for longer this time. As I said in my letter, there's a big conference on Monday. All the interpreters are needed.' He reached into his pocket. 'Look, I've brought you this. Call it a wedding present. Open it later.'

He handed Day an envelope on which his name was written in a handwriting he recognised from his student days at Cambridge. Ophelia's handwriting.

'Is this …?'

'Yes. Later, okay? When you're alone.'

'My God! It's good news?'

'I think so, or I wouldn't have given it to you today.'

'Of course.'

'I'll call you tomorrow before I leave for the airport, when you've had a chance to read it.'

They managed to talk of other things, but inwardly they were all preoccupied with the contents of the envelope. When Raj went to rejoin Jacques and Marie-Claude, he turned only once to give them a smile and a little wink.

'Can you resist opening it?' asked Helen in a low voice.

'He said to wait till we're alone…'

'Mmm, I know.'

They shared a small laugh, and it was only the approach of the violinist that prevented the opening of the envelope. They were about to find out who he was.

'Hello,' he said, putting the violin case on a low wall. 'I'm really sorry to turn up unexpectedly. I didn't know how to contact you. In Greece, I mean. So I just took a chance. I'm Joe. Joe Murray.'

It was a few seconds before Helen reacted.

'Murray? You're my *brother*?'

'Yes. Half-brother, at least.'

Day was even more surprised than Helen; he had never heard of a brother. Joe Murray saw his confusion and offered an explanation that he may have been preparing all afternoon.

'My mother - Helen's and mine - left Helen's father before I was born. She'd met my father.'

Helen was flushed, shaking her head.

'I was seven. Stupidly, I wrote to her before we got married; goodness knows what possessed me. She didn't reply, just like she didn't when I wrote to tell her that my father had died.'

'I'm really sorry,' said Joe, before Day could think what to say. 'She hasn't been well.'

'Not well? Did she even tell you about my letter?'

'Oh yes, I read your letter, and I wanted to come to your wedding myself, but I had no-one to look after Mum. I'm her carer. Your letter helped me reach a decision, actually. She needed proper care, and the doctor agreed. The trouble was, by the time everything was arranged, it was after your wedding and you seemed to be away. I just bought a ticket on impulse.'

The stunned silence was drawing out; Day had to reply for them both.

'You're welcome,' he said, 'and we loved your music.'

A smile finally came to Joe's face. With a grateful look to Day over his shoulder, he gave Helen an awkward hug.

'How long will you be on Naxos?' she said, when they drew apart.

'As long as I like. Mum's in a nursing home being properly looked after, and she doesn't know whether I'm there or not these days. I've renting a cheap room in Vivlos, not far from the port.'

He reached into the pocket of his shirt and handed her a piece of paper.

'My details are on here. Will you call me?'

Helen nodded.

'I'd really like to get to know you both. You're all the family I have left, actually.'

He picked up his violin case and walked away towards the taverna, not waiting for an answer.

'Well, that wasn't part of the plan, was it?' said Day. 'Are you all right?'

'Yes. I'm fine.'

"Did you recognise him?'

'No. I've never even seen a picture of him. The Murrays weren't part of my childhood, as you can imagine. My stepmother Margot brought me up, and I left home for Greece before I was eighteen.'

'Ah, yes, your Zissis years,' murmured Day, reflecting that he had never even seen a picture of his predecessor, the Greek playboy who was Helen's first husband. 'How do you really feel about Joe showing up?'

She woke from her thoughts and put her hand on his arm.

'None of that matters now. Not Joe, not Zissis.'

Back at the pergola, sweet delights were being placed on the marble serving table. There was a traditional Greek cake made to Anna's own recipe, moistened with a flavoursome orange syrup and strewn with slivers of sweetened orange rind. There were also *koulourakia* biscuits, Naxian marzipan specialities called *amygdalota*, and various dishes of homemade spoon sweets. The staff were taking orders for coffee.

Helen rejoined Aristos and Rania at their table, and Day wandered over to talk to Maria, Fabrizio and Peppino.

After about ten minutes he heard the light tapping of a spoon on the rim of a glass. Another speech, but one that he had half expected. He gazed across at Helen, who was pushing back her chair.

'I'm never short of something to say, as you know,' she began. 'I certainly wasn't going to miss this chance!'

There was some light drumming on the table from Alex Harding-Jones, and a murmur of appreciative laughter.

'I just want to add my voice to Martin's, and thank you all very much for being here. It really does mean such a lot to both of us. It's been wonderful for me to meet some of his friends for the first time and hear some rather interesting stories. Scott over there, who is the director who has to deal with Martin on set, has told me one or two very interesting anecdotes. Efi, and Maria, Jacques, Lizzie and Siobhan, it's been lovely to meet you and hear all your stories about my husband.'

Day, who was aware of eyes on him, obligingly pulled a face as if embarrassed.

'Of course, it works both ways. There are two people here who have met Martin for the first time today. My lovely friend, Suzanne, who is sitting over here - we've known each other since we were at school, can you believe? It's very special to me that she's here today. Thank you, dear old friend.'

'The other new face here today is my step-brother, Joe.'

She looked round for him, but Joe was nowhere to be seen.

'He's disappeared. Joe was our wonderful violinist.'

She was saved from saying more by the spontaneous applause.

'Perhaps we can persuade him to play for us again, before the dancing starts. Meanwhile, please enjoy your evening: there are delicious things for dessert and there's plenty of wine. And again, thank you all very much.'

She topped up her glass and walked over to join Day. The sun was setting, though its path lay behind a ridge of the Mount Fanari range. Its glow was infusing the haze above the rock with amber.

Peppino Berducci stood up to greet her with a certain Sicilian flourish, taking both her hands in his and then pulling out a chair for her.

'Signora Day! *Complimenti*! This man, your husband, is one of the people I respect most in the world!' he said. 'Martin, this is a beautiful lady, a lady of grace and intelligence. You must come to Sicily and be my guests.'

From somebody else, these effusive compliments might have been unwelcome, but Helen already felt comfortable with Peppino. Confidently sporting a bright, floral shirt, his thick, dark hair revealed traces of the silver that was beginning to take hold at the temples. He went on to tell her about his love of marble, painting a picture of the nature, colours and potential of the stone. Such was his enthusiasm and knowledge that Helen encouraged him to talk at length. By the time he had finished, the sky had filled with a purple softness and the afternoon had sunk into velvet, motionless night.

Day, meanwhile, though apparently listening, was savouring the fragrant air of the mountains. He had spoken to everyone and was feeling relaxed. Peppino excused himself and moved away to get some coffee, leaving them once again alone.

'Peppino's interesting, I like him,' she said, leaning into Day comfortably.

'I knew you would. One day we should take him up on that suggestion to go to Sicily.'

'Yes, we should do that.'

He took her hand.

'I'd really like to know what's in the letter from Ophelia. The dancing will start soon and we won't have a chance. I'm not sure I can wait. Can you?'

He had a point; the band had arrived and were already preparing to play.

A Greek Feast on Naxos

'All right, let's read it. Why don't we go and sit over there?'

There was a small bench at the far end of the terrace which was almost in darkness. A small lamp, set into the wall, would give them just enough light to read by. They sat down with their backs to the pergola, and Helen took the envelope out of her bag.

Day hesitated once he had the letter in his hand. From its weight he imagined it contained just a single sheet of paper. He gently prised it open.

Dearest Martin,

I wish I could have sent this to you before. I expect you've been worried about me, and I'm truly sorry for that, but I've been travelling for a long time.

I hope you've been able to forgive me for everything, and that you know how grateful I am and will always be for what you did. You freed me to move on. I couldn't have done it alone, either physically or emotionally. I lacked the courage. I couldn't bring myself to tell anyone what had happened all those years ago, the terrible events that you now know all about.

A few years ago, before I met you again, I did almost go to the police, because I was the only one left alive who knew the whole story, and that weighed heavily on me. I didn't do it, as you know. Instead I sometimes thought of taking my own life, but I couldn't do that either, so I simply drifted on, coming back to Naxos each year like a pilgrim.

Then, that August day, I saw you sitting at Diogenes bar. After so many years, there you were. The right person, the only *person who might be able to put things right, as far as that could ever be done. So I decided to put everything in your hands, gave you all the information I could, and I walked away. I left Greece, wandered about in the Middle East, and came here to Nepal, though not directly. I managed to find out first about your incredible success. You did it!*

The only thing I wanted then was to spend the rest of my life differently. Call it atonement. I needed to live somewhere more real than the ivory towers of the university, and to be useful. I've ended up here, working on a literacy programme in a village in Nepal. It's as different from my old life in Cambridge as it could possibly be, but it's so rewarding. The people are wonderful, and it feels good to end up in the country where Raj started life before he came to live with us as a child.

There's no more to say, really. I wish you a very happy life, Martin, and I'll always be grateful to you, and love you.

You and Helen are very good together; don't waste time, darling!

With love, Ophelia.

'So, now we know,' murmured Helen, seeing that Day could not speak. 'She's making reparation. Oh dear. She wasn't blameless, of course, but it was more of a tragedy than anything.'

She looked at him, but he was still staring at the letter. She put her arm round him and looked up into the night sky.

'Poor Ophelia,' she murmured. 'Everything she worked for all her life is gone. Her much-loved Cambridge, her friends, even her own son ... she's lost them all, maybe for ever. All because she loved somebody too much.'

Day was holding the letter open, but his eyes were now closed. The low light from the lamp fell on the side of his face.

'She wanted you to know where she is,' Helen whispered. 'She didn't want to leave you in that state of unknowing.'

He nodded. She gently took the letter from his fingers, folded it and replaced it in the envelope. As she tucked it back in her bag she caught sight of Raj, who was watching them from a little way away. He had seen them reading the letter, seen their reaction; there were three of them in the moment, which Helen found comforting.

'She's alive, and happy enough now, and fulfilled. It could have been so much worse, darling.'

He opened his eyes and blinked. The light of the moon stretched across the surface of the sea in a pathway that connected the terrace of the Agnanti with the horizon.

'Is Raj still here?' he said at last, his eyes still on the sea.

'Yes, he's here.'

The young Nepali, Ophelia's adopted son, saw Helen's look of appeal. He brought up a chair and sat down with them.

'You've read it,' he said. 'What did she tell you?'

'That she's teaching in Nepal,' said Day, and cleared his throat. 'She knows that we managed to succeed. Do you know any more, Raj?'

'Your letter was enclosed with one to me,' he said. 'She told me about her journey from Naxos, where she went and what happened on the way to Nepal. She was sorry for leaving without telling me, and I understand now. She also told me where she's living, so I'm going to see her.'

'That's great,' said Day, reviving. 'When?'

'Later this summer. I'll go for a couple of months. I'll give up my job: they won't give me enough time off. There's always work for interpreters.' He, too, looked out at the sea. 'You could give me a letter to take to her, if you want. No rush, plenty of time to think.'

'Of course. Thanks, we will.'

Raj hesitated.

'She asked me to tell you that you should allow your name to be associated with your discovery. She said she knows you're protecting her by keeping back your name, but she says that the archaeological record should be accurate. Does that make any sense to you?'

'Yes. I was her student, remember.'

Day was smiling now, almost as broadly as if she had just walked onto the terrace. At Cambridge, Ophelia had been both his tutor and his lover. She had been not much older than himself, and he had adored her. He had also listened to her. She was reminding him of a guiding principle of archaeology: the supreme importance of an object's recorded provenance. He had not needed reminding of it. He had simply made a decision to put a friend before a principle, and had convinced himself that he was right to refuse permission for his name to be associated with the discovery of the Kállos of Naxos, in order that Ophelia's part in it would never come to light.

Raj was still looking at him blankly.

'She means that every aspect of an archaeological discovery should ideally be placed on record. It's important that an ancient object is understood in its total context, and that we know the most we possibly can about it. Imagine if the treasures of Tutankhamun's tomb, for example, had been removed from the Royal Pyramid and sold off individually to buyers and museums across the world, without any information of where they'd been found. The most we could have said about some wonderful gold masterpiece would have been that it was a magnificent piece of craftsmanship from Ancient Egypt. We would have no chance to appreciate it as part of a specific royal burial, throwing light on our knowledge of a major ancient ruler, his importance underlined by the sheer amount and quality of the grave goods buried with him, and the many other things that could be learned about that society.

'Obviously, this discovery isn't on the scale of Tutankhamun's tomb, and the excavation, when it finally takes place, will be properly recorded. I've told the authorities all I know about it, everything except Ophelia's involvement. Withholding permission to publish my name means I can protect her.'

'I see. Well, it's your decision, Martin,' said Raj, 'and I understand why you made it. I'm just telling you what she said. Think about it.'

Day agreed to think about it. They sat together for another half hour, talking mostly about Raj's trip to Nepal. When he said goodbye, it felt rather like the end of the party., especially as Nick and Deppi left at the same time with the children. Then Dimitris announced that the dancing was about to begin.

A trio of Greek musicians set up and began to play. There were just enough Greeks among the guests to show the non-Greeks how to dance the famous *syrtaki*, with amusing results. It would not have been a Greek wedding without this moment, and everyone made the most of it. After the *syrtaki* there were slower dances, in a more English tradition. These were particularly enjoyed by the couples, and by those who seemed likely to get together.

Only when it was very late did Markos announce that the minibus had arrived for the guests staying at the Elias House and the nearby Taverna Ta Votsala. Ben,

A Celebration of Cuisine in the Cyclades from the author of The Naxos Mysteries

Suzanne, Alex and Kate, Scott, and Maurice left the Agnanti reluctantly. Thanasis and his family, Aristos and Rania, and Jacques and Marie-Claude, all took their leave too.

In the quiet that descended on the party after these departures, Dimitris discreetly began clearing the tables under the canopy. Day asked him if he knew where the violinist was.

'He left a little while ago. I called a taxi for him.'

'Perhaps he felt awkward,' said Helen, when she heard. 'I'll call him tomorrow.'

'Do you want him in your life?' Day ventured, after a little hesitation.

'I think so.'

The remaining guests moved two tables together and created a new seating area near the bougainvillea. They gathered up all the remaining bottles and jugs of wine, and settled down to enjoy what was left of the evening. Fabrizio was soon holding forth about the beauties of western Crete, where he was excavating in the area around Phaistos.

'Martin's coming out to Crete in a few weeks to do some filming. Isn't that right? Maria, you must come, too! How about it, Maria? Come to Crete!'

Maria told him she would, but in a light-hearted way which committed her to nothing. She stretched out her hand to invite Day to sit next to her. He looked for Helen, but she had gone to sit near Andreas and Fotini. There was a sudden eruption of laughter; he supposed that Lizzie and Siobhan were sharing more stories about his bachelor days.

So he took the chair next to Maria. She leaned in and kissed him lightly on the cheek.

'Congratulations, Martin *mou*,' she said quietly. 'I'm very happy for you. Thank you for inviting me, I've had a great time tonight. I've met more people than in the four years our family have lived on Naxos.'

Day grinned, glad now that she had come.

It was not only Maria who was happy. Fabrizio was talking with Peppino and Angelika as if they had known each other for ever. The quiet and studious Efi, who had recently lost her father, was relaxed and smiling, talking with Scott and Maurice. He put it all down to the magic of the Cyclades.

He caught Helen's eye. At the end of the night he would be very glad to go home to Filoti, where they could be alone together.

It was not time for that yet, however. Markos put a tray of glasses on the table and Dimitris appeared at Day's side with a bottle of *mastiha*, the traditional digestif from Chios island.

'With our compliments, Martin,' he murmured.

'Thanks, Dimitri. It's been a wonderful evening. Thank you all.'

Well pleased, Dimitris returned to the kitchen to enjoy his own dinner.

Day sat back with his glass of *mastiha*. Completely clear and chilled, its unique aroma was subtle, perfumed. He allowed a little of the liquid to dally on his tongue, and only gradually to reach the rest of his mouth. Its sweetness was balanced by an aromatic warmth on his palate that spread as he swallowed. He smiled to himself. *Mastiha* was truly in a class of its own, in his opinion. Some people loved it, some hated it, but Day was on the side of the lovers. It was the perfect way to end the evening.

Yet this did not feel like an ending at all. There were two of them now, and it felt like a new beginning. There was more to discover about Greek antiquity, more to learn about Naxos, and more to experience among the people of this island. Perhaps there would even be more adventures.

Yes, there would be more adventures. He was sure of that.

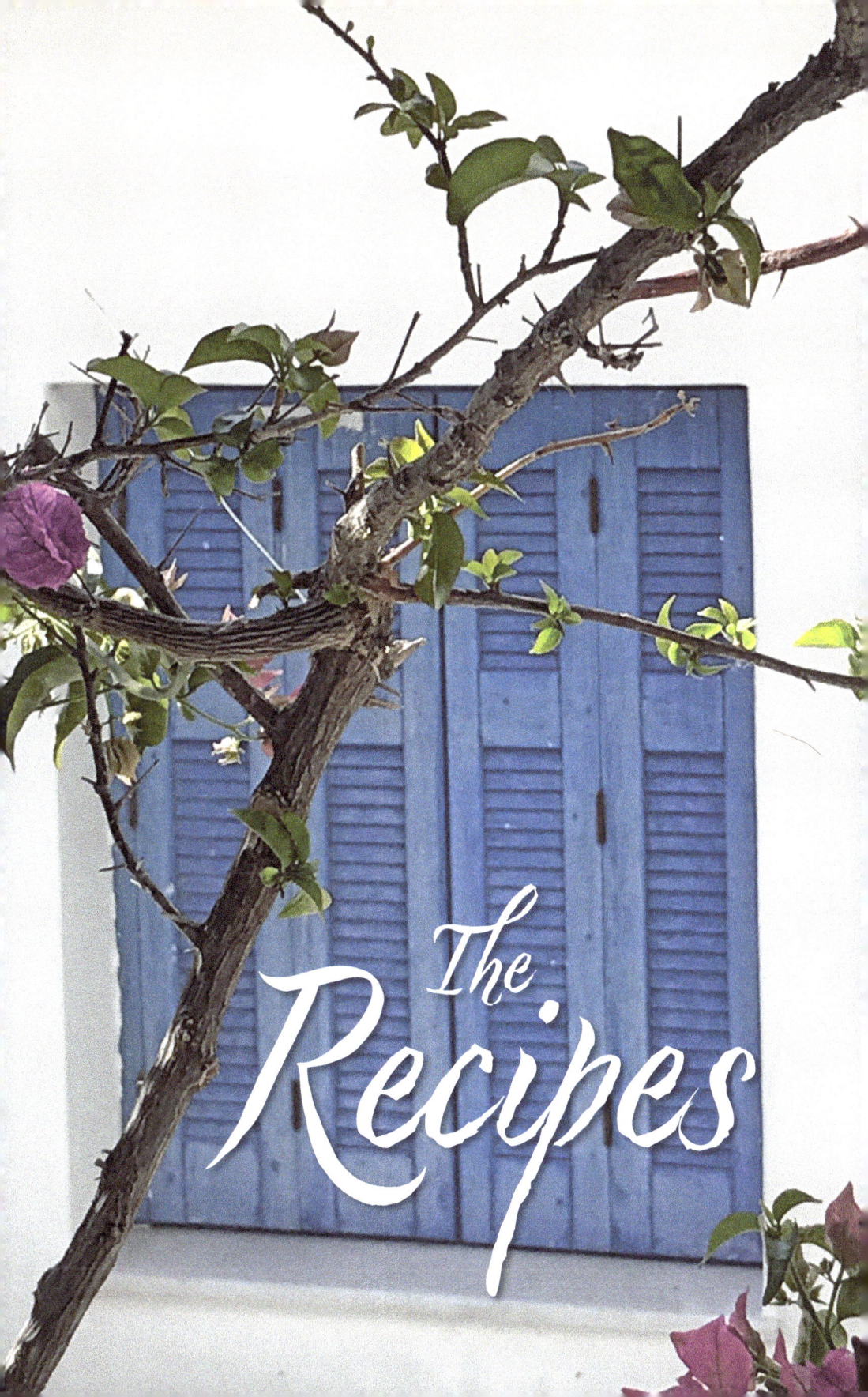

The Recipes

THE RECIPES

DIPS, PIES AND SALADS
Fava (Yellow Split Pea Dip)
Melitzanosalata (Aubergine Dip)
Eggplant 'Caviar' (Aubergine and Pomegranate Pâté)
Tyropitakia (Little Cheese Pies)
Pitarakia (Little Cheese Pies)
Horiatiki Salad (Traditional Greek Salad)
Two Other Salads found on Naxos
Beetroot Salad 'Axiotissa Style'
Tzatziki (Greek Yogurt Dip)

FRITTERS AND BALLS (Keftedes)
Keftedes (Small meatballs)
Domatokeftedes (Tomato balls)
Kolokythokeftedes (Courgette balls)
Fennel Fritters from 'Axiotissa'

THE MAIN COURSE
Arni Sto Fourno (Greek Roast Lamb)
Patates Fournou (Greek Roast Potatoes)
Yemista (Stuffed Tomatoes)
'Axiotissa' Stuffed Vegetables
Kalogeros (A Naxian speciality)

SWEET TREATS
Tou Yiaourtiou (Almond and Yogurt Cake with Citrus Syrup)
Koulourakia 'Methesmena' ('Tipsy' Koulourakia Biscuits)
Glika tou Koutaliou (Spoon sweets)

THE CHEFS

Some of the recipes here have been handed down from generation to generation, and there are many variations out there. Inevitably, as with everything cooked by our grandmothers, mothers and aunts, each family will have its preferred version. Some of the recipes have reached me this way.

Others are from named Greek cooks, who have kindly given me their permission to share them with you. Their cookery books include a great deal of interesting and informative text in addition to the recipes, and I urge you to consider buying them if you are a 'Greek Foodie'. All the details are given below.

Yiannis Vassilas owns Taverna Axiotissa on Naxos, close to Kastraki Beach. A more passionate advocate of good food than Yiannis would be very hard to find. **Aglaia Kremezi**'s books on Greek cuisine are well-known modern classics of Greek cookery. **The Friends of Paros and Antiparos** have compiled an excellent volume in three languages on the cuisine and culture of their islands, which neighbour Naxos and appear in several of the *Mysteries* because they, too, are favourite places of mine.

The speciality called Kalogeros (it appears in *The Reach of the Past*) is a Naxian recipe that you can find on the website **Eat Yourself Greek**, which is also a good place to read about other tasty treats. I am also delighted to include recipes and advice from my friends in the Cyclades, **Anastasia Peristeraki** and **Jean Polyzoides**, who live on Naxos and Paros respectively.

> **Yiannis Vassilas**: *Around the Cooking Pot of Axiotissa* (2019) ***www.axiotissa.com***
> **Aglaia Kremezi**: *The Foods of the Greek Islands* (2000) ***www.aglaiakremezi.com***
> **The Friends of Paros and Antiparos**: *Cycladic Culture and Gastronomy*
> **Eat Yourself Greek**: Greek cuisine ***www.eatyourselfgreek.com***
> **Anastasia Peristeraki** and her family own Kedros Villas Hotel, Naxos
> ***www.kedrosvillas.gr*** (Kedros Villas appears as Yiasemi Villas in
> *The Disappearance of Ophelia Blue*)
> **Jean Polyzoides** is a long-term resident of Paros and my friend

FAVA
Yellow Split Pea Dip

Serve slightly warm, with crusty fresh bread

INGREDIENTS
500g yellow split peas, rinsed in a sieve and drained
1 onion, chopped
1 bay leaf
Salt
Juice of 1 lemon
Greek extra virgin olive oil
Dried oregano

TO GARNISH
Fava is usually garnished with chopped spring (or gentle) onions. Caramelised onions can be used if preferred. A few capers are a popular addition in the Cyclades.

INSTRUCTIONS
Boil the split peas with the onion, bay leaf and a little salt in a non-stick saucepan over medium heat. Skim off the scum.

When the split peas are soft but still retain some liquid, take off the heat and remove the bay leaf. If a good purée has been achieved, there is no need to use a food processor, but it will depend on the split peas you have used. The fava should be smooth and creamy but not too stiff and thick.

Add the lemon juice, a little olive oil and the oregano, and serve in a small bowl, garnished as suggested above.

MELITZANOSALATA
Aubergine Dip

Serve at room temperature, with crusty bread

INGREDIENTS
2 large aubergines
2 garlic cloves, crushed
1 small onion, chopped
125ml Greek olive oil
1 tbsp red wine vinegar
1 tbsp lemon juice
Salt and black pepper
2 tbsp chopped parsley (optional)

Pre-heat oven to 200°C (180°C for fan oven)
Prepare a lined baking tray

INSTRUCTIONS
Wash and dry the aubergines and roast on a lined baking sheet till soft and the skin has charred.

Allow to cool until easy to handle, then halve lengthways and discard some of the seedy centre.

Transfer the flesh to a sieve and allow to drain. This is to avoid your dip being too wet.

Place the flesh and the rest of the ingredients in a food processor and blend to achieve the consistency of dip you prefer. Alternatively, you may be able to achieve better results with a fork. A smooth and creamy dip is traditional, rather than a purée.

Serve in a small bowl.

A Celebration of Cuisine in the Cyclades from the author of The Naxos Mysteries

EGGPLANT 'CAVIAR'
Aubergine and Pomegranate Pâté

Recipe by Yiannis Vassilas of Taverna Axiotissa

INGREDIENTS
4 globe eggplants (aubergines)
1 garlic clove, finely chopped
1 handful of walnuts, finely chopped
Some fresh spearmint, finely chopped
1 level tsp cumin
2 tbsp good-quality, fruity olive oil
1 tsp good-quality balsamic vinegar
Seeds of 1 pomegranate
Salt and coarsely-ground black pepper

INSTRUCTIONS
Prick the eggplants with a fork and roast them whole on a grill (or ideally in a wood-fired oven, if available).

When cooked through, peel away the skins and finely chop the flesh.

Blend together with the other ingredients except the pomegranate seeds. You may do this in a food processor, but take care not to end up with a creamy paste.

Serve on toasted bread and sprinkle with pomegranate seeds.

TYROPITAKIA
Little Cheese Pies

As made by Jean Polyzoides

INGREDIENTS

One pack of frozen Filo pastry (10 sheets), thawed in the fridge. Allow to reach room temperature in its packaging before handling.
125g Greek Feta cheese
125g Mizithra cheese (you could substitute with Ricotta or crumbly curd cheese)
2 large eggs, beaten
1 tbsp chopped fresh herbs (mint, dill or parsley)
Ground black pepper, and a little salt (Remember, Feta is quite salty already)
125g unsalted butter, melted

Pre-heat oven to 200° C (180°C for fan oven)
Prepare a greased baking tray

INSTRUCTIONS

Mash together the cheeses, eggs, herbs, salt and pepper in a bowl.

Cut the pastry sheets into long strips about 3 inches wide.

Brush each strip with butter (Filo contains no fat).

Put a heaped teaspoon of the mixture onto one end of each strip and fold over to make a triangle. Keep folding over until you have enclosed the cheese in the entire strip and formed a parcel. Brush your parcel with more butter, and put onto greased baking tray.

Continue with the rest of the pastry until you have used up your ingredients.

Bake in pre-heated oven for about 15 minutes until light golden brown and crispy.

They should be eaten immediately while still warm from the oven.

A Celebration of Cuisine in the Cyclades from the author of The Naxos Mysteries

PITARAKIA
(More) Little Cheese Pies

Recipe from *Cycladic Culture and Gastronomy*

INGREDIENTS

FOR THE PASTRY
500g flour
2tbsp lemon juice or raki
2 tbsp olive oil
Salt and water

FOR THE FILLING
250g Xinomyzithra cheese (or crumbly goats cheese)
3 tbsp natural Greek yogurt
1 egg
Mint, pepper

INSTRUCTIONS
Prepare the pastry: In a large bowl combine all the ingredients for the dough and add the required amount of water until it no longer sticks to the sides of the bowl.

Cover the bowl with cling film, and let it rest in the fridge.

Make the filling: Beat the egg lightly, and stir in the cheese, yogurt and herbs.

Make up the pies: Roll out the pastry and cut into about 5 square sheets.

Put a teaspoon of the filling in the centre of each sheet and fold it to enclose the cheese mixture.

Fry the pies in hot oil.

A Greek Feast on Naxos

HORIATIKI SALATA
Traditional Greek Salad

Use the most flavoursome ingredients you can find!

INGREDIENTS
4 large ripe tomatoes, cut into chunks, not slices ('heritage' tomatoes are expensive but tasty)
¼ of a large cucumber, or the equivalent, part-peeled, cut into chunks
1 green pepper, prepared and cut into pieces
1 small onion, preferably mild white type, sliced and cut to taste
12-16 Kalamata olives, which must be left whole
200g Greek Feta cheese
Dried oregano, ideally Greek 'rigani'
Greek extra virgin olive oil

INSTRUCTIONS
Prepare all the vegetables. In a Greek salad, the ingredients are cut into quite large chunks, not cubes or slices, and the olives are left whole.

Arrange the tomatoes, cucumber, and green pepper in a serving bowl, and top with onion slices and olives. Do not toss your salad.

Place the Feta cheese on top in a single piece (if for an individual portion) or cubed (if to share), and dress it with a drizzle of oil and a sprinkle of dried oregano.

Leave the olive oil within reach of your guests, and serve with crusty slices of bread rather than pitta or flat bread.

A Celebration of Cuisine in the Cyclades from the author of The Naxos Mysteries

TWO OTHER SALADS
Found on Naxos by the Author

'APOLLON' SALAD

INGREDIENTS
Cucumber, tomato, thin slices of white onion, black olives, capers, crumbly cheese (Xinomyzithra), oregano, and a light dressing of oil and vinegar.

(Enjoyed at Apollon Taverna, Chora, Naxos)

'FILARAKIA' SALAD

INGREDIENTS
Tomato, green pepper, red pepper, cooked potato chunks, cucumber, black olives, red onion slices, capers, sliced beetroot, a small amount of shredded lettuce as a base. Add your own delicious olive oil.

(Enjoyed at Filarakia Taverna, Chora, Naxos)

BEETROOT SALAD 'AXIOTISSA STYLE'
Recipe by Yiannis Vassilas of Taverna Axiotissa

INGREDIENTS
6-7 small beetroots of similar size (3-4cm dia.)
1 handful walnuts
1 small handful fresh spearmint
Dash of good quality vinegar
1-2 tbsp olive oil
1 tbsp honey (optional)
2-3 garlic cloves
2tbsp Greek (strained) yogurt
Pinch of salt
A few shavings of Xinotyro cheese (you could substitute with Chèvre)

INSTRUCTIONS
Wash the beets and boil in a pot of water. When tender, rinse with cold water to cool, then peel by hand. Cut into any shape you like, and put in a bowl with vinegar and salt to season.

Blend the olive oil, yogurt, spearmint and garlic (and honey if using), in a blender.

Empty this purée into the bowl of beets, and mix well.

Taste and adjust seasoning as necessary.

Sprinkle with the walnuts and top with cheese shavings.

Yiannis talks about BEETROOT:
'Before cooking beets, make sure they are the same size - as far as possible - so that they cook at the same rate. Also make sure to buy them with their leaves still attached; first of all, they will last longer, and you can also use the perfectly edible, sweet and tender leaves. And a final reminder: the smaller the beet, the sweeter and tastier it is. The beet salad I serve at Axiotissa, tweaked and improved over the years, makes a lovely combination with grilled or fried fish.'

A Celebration of Cuisine in the Cyclades from the author of The Naxos Mysteries

TZATZIKI
Yogurt, Cucumber & Garlic Dip

INGREDIENTS

400g Greek (strained) yogurt, full fat
1 large garlic clove, crushed
1 tbsp white wine vinegar
1 tbsp Greek olive oil
1 large cucumber, peeled, seeded and diced finely (or grated)
2 tsp fresh dill, chopped (some people choose mint)
Salt and black pepper

INSTRUCTIONS

Remove excess moisture from the diced cucumber. It is important to do this thoroughly, to avoid a tzatziki that is too watery.

Put all the ingredients in a large bowl and mix well.

Cover and chill in the fridge, ideally overnight but for at least an hour, to allow the full flavour to emerge

Meat Keftedes with Tzatziki

A Greek Feast on Naxos

KEFTEDES
Small Meatballs made with Beef and Herbs

Based on a recipe of Jean Polyzoides

INGREDIENTS
500-600g minced beef (or mixture beef/pork/veal)
2 onions, finely chopped
1 garlic clove, crushed
150g stale bread
A little wine, olive oil or ouzo
1 egg, beaten
Handful of fresh parsley, mint or spearmint, chopped
1 tsp Greek dried oregano
Salt and black pepper
Plain flour for dusting (if using)
Olive oil for frying

INSTRUCTIONS
Soak the bread in the wine, oil or ouzo, and then squeeze it very well.

Pull into small pieces and put in a large bowl with the meat, onion, garlic, egg, herbs and seasoning. Mix well with your hands to combine thoroughly.

Cover with cling film and chill in the fridge for an hour (or overnight).

When ready to cook, take small pieces of the meat mixture and roll into balls the size of walnuts or golfballs.

Either: Dust in flour, shake off excess and fry in batches in hot oil in a large frying pan until browned all over. Drain on kitchen paper.

Or: Oven-cook your meatballs on a non-stick sheet, without dredging them in flour but lightly brushing them with olive oil.

Serve with tzatziki (see recipe).

A Celebration of Cuisine in the Cyclades from the author of The Naxos Mysteries

DOMATOKEFTEDES
Tomato Balls #1

INGREDIENTS

4 tomatoes, the most flavourful you can find (Do not peel, or discard the seeds)
Optional for English kitchen - A small jar of sun-dried tomatoes, finely chopped, is good to add if your fresh tomatoes are not fully ripe, to improve the flavour of your keftedes
2 tbsp onion (or spring onions), grated or very finely chopped
¼ tsp cinnamon
2-3 tbsp fresh mint, or combination mint and parsley, finely chopped
1tbsp fresh dill, chopped
1 tbsp dried Greek oregano
Salt and black pepper
350ml plain flour, seasoned with salt and pepper
Olive oil for frying

INSTRUCTIONS

Chop the tomatoes (and the sun-dried if using), and put in a bowl with the grated onion, cinnamon, herbs, oregano and seasoning. Mix well.

Mix in the flour and form into balls or patties. Refrigerate uncovered to firm up.

The above can be done as much as a day ahead of time.

Heat oil in a frying pan, and cook the patties in small batches, allowing them to brown on all sides, about 3 minutes.

Drain on kitchen paper and serve warm.

These vegetable patties are delicious warm with a dip or a little Greek yogurt.

DOMATOKEFTEDES
Tomato Balls #2

Another method. Try both!

INGREDIENTS
3 ripe tomatoes
125g plain flour
Handful fresh spearmint, chopped
1 onion, grated
1 tbsp baking powder
1 tsp dried oregano
A little chopped fresh basil if desired.
Salt and pepper

Olive oil and sunflower oil for frying

INSTRUCTIONS
Peel tomatoes, remove seeds, squeeze to remove some of the juice, and leave in a sieve to drain.

Chop finely.

Place tomatoes in a large bowl and add all the other ingredients except the sunflower oil. Combine well and add a little flour if you think the tomatoes are too wet. Place in the fridge for 30 minutes.

Heat the sunflower oil in a frying pan till hot, and add flattened spoonfuls of the tomato mixture, a few at a time, till golden on both sides. Dry on kitchen paper and serve on a small plate while still warm.

KOLOKYTHOKEFTEDES
Courgette Balls

Thanks to Jean Polyzoides for this recipe

INGREDIENTS
4 large courgettes
½ red onion, chopped
1 garlic clove, finely chopped
3 tbsp fresh dill, finely chopped
2 tbsp fresh mint, finely chopped
1 cup good quality Greek Feta cheese
Plain flour
2 small eggs, beaten
Flour and olive oil for frying

INSTRUCTIONS
Grate the courgettes into a sieve and sprinkle with salt, and press with a weight to bring out the water (at least half an hour). Ensure the courgettes are as dry as possible.

Place the courgettes in a bowl with the herbs, onion and garlic, crumbled Feta and beaten eggs. Mix well, adding a little flour if necessary to bind the mixture together.

Leave in fridge for at least 30 minutes, then form into flattened balls.

Heat some olive oil in a frying pan until very hot and fry for 2-3 minutes on each side. Remove with a slotted spoon onto kitchen paper. Continue with the rest of the fritter mixture, keeping them warm.

Serve accompanied by a serving of tzatziki.

FENNEL FRITTERS
Recipe by Yiannis Vassilas of Taverna Axiotissa

INGREDIENTS
1 cup of fennel leaves, finely chopped
1 onion, finely chopped
Rustic yellow flour (quantity, see recipe)
Salt and coarsely ground black pepper
2 tbsp ouzo
Feta cheese, optional

INSTRUCTIONS
Combine all the ingredients to form a moderately thick batter. Add the flour sparingly, because if the batter is too thick, the fritters will leave a bread-like taste in the mouth.

You can also grate some Feta cheese into the mixture if you like; just make sure to use less salt in this case.

Form into fritters.

Fry in a generous amount of olive oil, though not enough to cover the fritters, over a medium heat.

Yiannis talks about FENNEL

'Fennel is one of my favourite spring herbs. Wild fennel sprouts just about everywhere in the fields of Naxos, so I use it like there's no tomorrow in the restaurant's spring menu. One whiff of wild fennel was all it took for me to forget dill, its close relative, forever.

'I gather lots of fennel in spring and dry it, so as not to run out during the summer. It is an ideal match for some fish, including gilt-head bream, sea bass and sargo (white sea bream), which can be baked on a bed of fennel or stuffed with plenty of fennel sprigs. Other dishes that greatly benefit from fennel are meat-stuffed zucchini and, of course, rice-stuffed vine leaves.'

ARNI STO FOURNO
Greek Roast Lamb

Greek lamb is smaller than the lamb we buy in Britain, so ask your butcher for a small, tender joint

INGREDIENTS
A leg of lamb on the bone
1 garlic, all cloves peeled and sliced
2 onions, peeled and quartered
Juice of 2 lemons
2 fl. oz. olive oil
2 tbsp dried Greek oregano
Salt and black pepper
2 sprigs fresh rosemary

Pre-heat oven to 180°C (160°C for fan oven)

INSTRUCTIONS for the MARINADE (You could do this the previous day)
Make many slits in the surface of the meat with the point of a sharp knife and insert slivers of garlic into each. Put the joint in the roasting pan. Combine olive oil and lemon juice and pour it over the lamb. Season with salt, pepper and oregano. Leave to marinate in the fridge overnight, and bring to room temperature before you start to cook.

INSTRUCTIONS
Tuck the sprigs of rosemary and the chunks of onion round the lamb and add 8 fl. oz. water. Season again if liked. Cover tightly with silver foil, making sure the foil isn't touching the lamb (you can insert a sheet of greaseproof paper if you like).

Roast for 3 hours until lamb is almost falling off the bone. Remove foil for a further 30 minutes, watching to prevent over-cooking.

Serve with roast potatoes and tzatziki.

A Celebration of Cuisine in the Cyclades from the author of The Naxos Mysteries

PATATES FOURNOU
Greek Roast Potatoes

Martin Day loves these ...

INGREDIENTS
1.5kg baking potatoes, peeled and cut into pieces (about 4cm)
4 garlic cloves, chopped
3 fl.oz. Greek olive oil
2 tsp dried Greek oregano
Juice of 1 lemon
Salt and black pepper

THE GARNISH
Handful fresh oregano, chopped

Pre-heat oven to 200°C (180°C for fan oven)*
Times are approximate; it will depend on the size of your potatoes.

INSTRUCTIONS
Place the prepared potatoes in a deep roasting dish in a single layer and add the garlic, oil, lemon juice, salt, pepper and dried oregano. Mix well to combine. If liked, try adding chunks of the squeezed lemon in among the potatoes.

Roast at 200°C for 15 minutes, then remove and add 4 fl. oz. water, turn potatoes gently and bake for a further 10 minutes. Toss again and bake another 15 minutes till cooked through.

*ALTERNATIVE COOKING METHODS
1. Prepare your oven to 180°C instead and cover the baking dish with silver foil, having dotted your potatoes with butter. After an hour, uncover and cook for a further 30 minutes, turning to prevent sticking, until potatoes are soft and lightly browned.
2. I have also seen Greek friends make this dish entirely under the grill.

Serve with a sprinkling of fresh oregano, and remember to remove any pieces of roast lemon.

YEMISTA
Stuffed Baked Tomatoes

(The meat can be left out of this recipe and the amount of rice increased)
Recipe adapted from one by Jean Polyzoides

INGREDIENTS
6 'beefsteak' tomatoes
Salt
1 large onion, finely chopped
3 garlic cloves, finely chopped
250g beef mince (or lamb mince) if using
The pulp from the beefsteak tomatoes
Two regular-sized tomatoes, chopped
1 small bunch each of mint and parsley, chopped
100g risotto rice
40g pine nuts or roasted, chopped hazelnuts
40g currants or sultanas
6 fl. oz. vegetable stock
Olive oil

Pre-heat oven to 190°C (170°C for fan oven)

INSTRUCTIONS
Slice the tops off the tomatoes, retaining them. Remove the pulp, sprinkle with salt, and arrange in a baking dish.

Soften the onions and garlic in olive oil then add the mince. Cook gently till lightly browned. Add all the other filling ingredients *using half the stock*, cover and cook until the liquid has been absorbed. Add a little more stock if necessary. The rice should not be soft at this stage.

Carefully fill the empty tomatoes with stuffing to about two thirds full and replace their lids. Pour the rest of the stock around them, and drizzle with 2-3 tbsp olive oil.

Oven bake for about an hour until the meat and rice are cooked and the vegetables are tender. The lids of the tomatoes are traditionally preferred crisp and browned. Serve warm.

A Celebration of Cuisine in the Cyclades from the author of The Naxos Mysteries

'AXIOTISSA' STUFFED VEGETABLES
Another version of Yemista
(Makes enough for a party!)

Recipe by Yiannis Vassilas in *Around the Cooking Pot of Axiotissa*

INGREDIENTS
12 medium tomatoes
2 medium peppers
2 eggplants (aubergines)
3-4 medium potatoes, cut into wedges
2 tbsp dry breadcrumbs
500g ripe tomatoes, grated* and drained
3 tsp good-quality tomato paste
250ml olive oil

FOR THE FILLING
2 medium onions
1 handful black raisins
30g pine nuts
1 bunch parsley
3-4 tbsp fresh spearmint
2 tsp sugar
80g Arseniko or spicy Graviera cheese, diced (optional)
400g long-grain rice or coarse bulgar wheat or sour trahana**
Salt and pepper

* Tomatoes are often grated in Greek cuisine, but finely chopping them gives a similar result.
** Trahana is available online in the UK, including a vegan version.

Pre-heat oven to 200°C (180°C for fan oven)
You will need a large, deep-sided baking pan

INSTRUCTIONS
Wash the vegetables to be stuffed, and use a sharp knife to open them up as follows:

Peppers: Cut the tops off them, scoop out the seeds and discard, but keep the fleshy top part of the peppers where the seeds were attached.

Eggplants: Cut a thin, lengthwise slice off each one to give them a boat-like shape, or keep them intact and just create lid-like openings by cutting off their bottoms. In either case, scoop out the flesh and reserve in a bowl.

Tomatoes: Open up the tomatoes in a similar manner by cutting off their tops or bottoms. Scoop out the flesh carefully with a teaspoon, taking care not to rip the skin, to prevent the filling from spilling out.

Finely chop the flesh of all the vegetables and combine in a large bowl.

Finely chop the onions, spearmint and parsley, and add them to the chopped vegetables.

Add the rice (or bulgar wheat or sour trahana), the pine nuts and raisins, and ¾ of the olive oil. Season with salt and pepper, add the cheese if you are using it, and the sugar. Blend well, taste for salt, add a little more if necessary.

Fill the tomatoes, eggplants and peppers with the mixture, and arrange them neatly in the pan. Season the potato wedges with salt and pepper, and arrange them carefully among the stuffed vegetables. Combine the grated tomatoes with the tomato paste and pour the mixture among the vegetables. Scatter any left-over filling in the pan.

Add the rest of the olive oil to the pan, replace tops on the vegetables, lightly season the tops with salt, sprinkle with the dry breadcrumbs, and bake in a pre-heated oven at 200°C for at least 2 hours, until the tomato lids are toasty brown.

> Yiannis explains about different fillings:
> 'Rice based fillings are more grainy; fillings with bulgar wheat tend to have a thicker, creamy but fluffy texture, as well as a more distinctive flavour. Sour trahana stuffed vegetables fall into a category of their own. You can always mix and match ingredients, though, especially sour trahana with bulgar wheat in equal portions.'

KALOGEROS
A Naxian Speciality with Meat, Aubergine and Cheese

Recipe with thanks to Eat Yourself Greek

INGREDIENTS
For the Beef Stew
1kg beef, cut into chunks
1 onion, finely chopped
300ml tomatoes, chopped or grated (fresh, ripe tomatoes)
1 tbsp tomato paste
100ml olive oil
Salt and pepper to taste
Pinch of cinnamon
Pinch of sugar
Water

For the Aubergines
6 large aubergines
2 large ripe tomatoes, sliced
Naxos Graviera or Gruyere cheese
Olive oil
Salt, pepper, and a pinch of cinnamon

INSTRUCTIONS

Heat up a heavy-bottomed casserole and brown the beef in a tablespoon of olive oil. Follow with the finely chopped onion and cook until translucent.

Add the chopped tomatoes, tomato paste, sugar, cinnamon, salt and pepper and cook for approximately 1½ hours on low-medium heat.

There are two ways to prepare the aubergines: baked, or shallow fried.

If you bake them: Cut in half and scar the flesh of each half diagonally, from left to right and then right to left to create diamond-shaped cuts. Add a bit of salt, brush with olive oil and bake at 180°C for about 15 minutes.

If you fry them: Slice them thickly and shallow fry in a bit of olive oil, 2-3 minutes each side. Keep the oven going at 180°C, if you are baking the aubergines or preheat it at 180°C to continue.

When the beef stew is ready, take each half of the baked aubergines and push the flesh with a spoon to create a cup. Fill each half with beef stew and two generous tablespoons of tomato sauce. If you fried your aubergines, place two slices and top with the cooked beef and a generous helping of sauce. Finish with slices of cheese or grated Gruyere. Place in a deep baking dish and bake for 5-7 minutes until the cheese has melted.

Kalogeros is best served hot, straight from the oven.

A Celebration of Cuisine in the Cyclades from the author of The Naxos Mysteries

TOU YIAOURTIOU
Almond and Yogurt Cake with Citrus Syrup

Recipe by Aglaia Kremezi in *The Foods of the Greek Islands*

INGREDIENTS
1 cup sugar
3 large eggs, separated
2 tbsp unsalted butter, softened
1 cup Greek strained yogurt
1 cup fine semolina
1 cup all-purpose (plain) flour
2 tsp baking powder
⅔ cup brandy
Grated zest of 1 lemon
1 cup unblanched almonds, coarsely chopped

FOR THE SYRUP
1½ cups sugar (or 1 cup sugar plus 3 tbsp honey, or 4-5 tbsp marmalade)
1¼ cups water
Whole zest from ½ lemon removed in strips with a vegetable peeler
3-4 tbsp brandy

Pre-heat oven to 200°C (180°C for fan oven)
Grease a 10-inch round or springform cake tin

INSTRUCTIONS
Set aside 2 tbsp of the sugar. In a large bowl, with an electric mixer, beat the remaining sugar with the egg yolks until light-coloured (2-3 minutes). Beat in the butter, yogurt and semolina.

Sift together the flour and baking powder. Beat flour mixture into the egg-yolk mixture with the brandy and the lemon zest.

In a large bowl, with clean beaters, beat the egg whites until they form soft peaks. Fold them into the batter. Pour the batter into the prepared tin, shake gently to even the surface, and sprinkle with the almonds. Press them lightly with a spatula so they are almost completely submerged in the batter. Sprinkle with the reserved 2tbsp sugar.

Bake for about 40 minutes, or until the cake is golden brown on top and a cocktail stick inserted in the top comes out clean.

MEANWHILE make the syrup.

Stir the sugar (or sugar and honey, but if using marmalade do not add it yet), water and lemon peel together in a small saucepan and bring to the boil. Reduce the heat to low and simmer for 5 minutes. Remove from the heat. If you are using marmalade, add it now. Add the brandy.

AS SOON AS YOU REMOVE THE CAKE FROM THE OVEN, remove the lemon zest from the syrup and very slowly spoon the syrup evenly over the cake, covering the entire surface. Let it cool completely before serving. Store at room temperature.

Tou Yiaourtiou means 'made with yogurt'.

There are many other delicious recipes for Greek cakes in which the cake is soaked in a fruit or spice syrup. One of my favourites is called Portokalopita (*portokalo*: orange, *pita*: cake or pie). This is made with filo pastry, which you allow to dry out before crumbling it up and using it as you would use flour, finally covering the cake with a rich orange syrup while it is still warm.

KOULOURAKIA METHISMENA
'Tipsy' Sweet Cookies with Orange and Cinnamon

Recipe by Aglaia Kremezi from *The Foods of the Greek Islands*

INGREDIENTS
2½ cups all-purpose flour
½ cup whole wheat flour
1½ tbsp grated orange zest
1½ tsp baking soda
1 tsp ground cinnamon
¼ tsp salt
1 cup sugar
½ cup olive oil (or olive oil and sunflower oil)
⅔ cup freshly-squeezed orange juice
½ cup grappa or vodka

Pre-heat oven to 180°C (160°C for fan oven)

INSTRUCTIONS
In the food processor, pulse together the flours, orange zest, baking soda, cinnamon and salt.

In a large bowl, beat ½ cup of the sugar and the oil with an electric blender till well blended.

With the motor running, pour the orange juice, alcohol and sugar/oil mixture into the processor. Process until a smooth, oily, elastic dough forms; do not over-process.

Turn the dough out onto a lightly floured work surface and knead briefly, adding more flour if dough is too sticky. Divide dough into 8 pieces. Work with one piece of dough at a time, keeping the remaining dough covered with cling film. Roll each piece of dough into a 24-inch long rope, cut each rope into 8 lengths, then roll each slice into a 7-inch long rope. Shape each rope into a ring, pressing the ends together to seal. Repeat with all the dough.

Spread the remaining sugar on a plate. Press one side of each ring into the sugar, and place the rings an inch apart (sugar side up) on ungreased baking trays.

Bake cookies in batches for 30 minutes or until light golden and crisp. Transfer to a rack to cool, then store in airtight containers for up to 3 months.

GLIKA TOU KOUTALIOU
Traditional Spoon Sweets

Recipe from Anastasia Peristeraki of Kedros Villas, Naxos

INGREDIENTS
1kg seedless white grapes
Sugar, 500g or more depending on sourness of grapes
1 cup water
Juice of half a lemon
A bunch of arbaroriza leaves* (or substitute a vanilla or cinnamon stick)

INSTRUCTIONS
Prepare two sterile jars for your spoon sweets.

Wash and drain the grapes. In a large saucepan, place a cup of water and the sugar, and heat until the sugar has dissolved (5-10 minutes).

Add the grapes and arbaroriza leaves, and lower the heat. Cook for 35-40 minutes, stirring constantly. Skim off the foam that forms on the top. Try not to break up the fruit; it should remain whole.

Leave the mixture for 24 hours, and then add a tablespoon of lemon juice and remove any remaining arbaroriza leaves. Boil for another 10 minutes. While it is hot, pour the mixture into warmed jars, seal well, and store upside down until they have cooled completely.

> *** ARBARORIZA**
> This mysterious ingredient is *Pelargonium graveolens*, the scented-leaved geranium. In Greece it is called arbaroriza, and, of course, it grows happily in that climate. It has a perfumed, incense-like quality, and it is used in Greek cuisine in jams and spoon sweets. You can obtain the plant yourself in the UK from Norfolk Herbs (norfolkherbs.co.uk) and other vendors, at reasonable cost, and grow as you would any other tender herb or houseplant. Make sure the herb you purchase is clearly marked as for culinary use.

Literally 'sweets of the spoon', these delicacies are traditionally served on a teaspoon with coffee and a glass of water as a gesture of Greek hospitality, *filoxenia*. They are made with a wide variety of fruits and nuts.

THE FOOD PARADISE OF NAXOS

In Antiquity, Naxos was a fortunate island. It was fertile and productive, self-sufficient in food and had a reliable supply of fresh water. This made it powerful among the Aegean islands. There was also enough food to spare for trading, and the Naxians did so effectively from an early period. Archaeologists have discovered containers which once held Naxian wine in the excavated site of the Palace of Knossos on Crete, the main centre of the Minoan culture; there is also evidence that a variety of produce was traded to the ancient settlement of Akrotiri on Thera (modern Santorini).

Today, Naxos continues to be a highly successful producer of food, wine and spirits. The fertile area called the Tragea, near Halki in the centre of the island, is renowned for olive-growing, and for its fruit and agriculture. It is watered by springs, which in the Cycladic summer is essential. Around the village of Melanes, too, the many natural springs account for the lush vegetation which astonishes those who visit the famous Kouros. The three villages which make up Potamia, another central community, are renowned for their wine, honey, fruit and vegetables: the soil there is watered by a river (*potamia* is the Greek word for rivers). The only real danger is wild fires, which sadly can devastate the farmland and ruin livelihoods. Fishing boats leave from Chora and Agia Anna, and return with their catches in the morning of the following day.

Wine is produced in many places on Naxos, though it is not a large industry as it is on some of the islands. In the shops on Naxos you will mostly find bottled wine from neighbouring islands. Santa Anna Winery in Potamia offers visitors a tasting experience, and don't be afraid to try the house wine in your chosen taverna, ordered by the litre. *Ena tetarto krasi* means a quarter-litre jug of wine, and *ena misokilo* means a half-litre. It may encourage you to enjoy, like Martin Day, fresh wine 'from the barrel'.

Potatoes and tomatoes, among other vegetables, are outstandingly tasty on Naxos. If you are self-catering during your visit, you can buy them for yourself; in any restaurant, though, you can experience the delight of all the vegetables and herbs grown on Naxos simply by ordering a local salad, the fried or roasted Naxian potatoes, or the crispy fried vegetables.

Find out more about Naxian produce in the following pages.

FAMOUS NAXIAN CHEESES

Naxian Graviera
The name of this pale yellow cheese is literally a transliteration of 'Gruyère', but the texture and flavour can differ a great deal depending on how and for how long the cheese has been aged, which can be anything from months to several years. When young, it is quite sweet and mild; as it matures, it becomes nutty and piquant. This more mature cheese is also more crumbly, but just as delicious. Naxian Graviera is internationally recognised and was given PDO (Protected Designation of Origin) status in 1996.

Arseniko (Naxian Kefalotyri)
This delicious, piquant cheese is recognisable by its dark rind and strong aroma. Its name means 'male', as Thanasis teases Martin Day in *The Reach of the Past*. During the early stage of its creation, it is placed in small basket-like moulds which create the ridges on the exterior of the cheese that help us to identify it. It is used in the Naxian dish 'Kalogeros', for which I've given you a recipe, and is also fried as a *saganaki* (deep-fried cheese), though it is also delicious eaten in your fingers with a glass of wine.

Myzithra and *Xinomyzithra*
Myzithra is a whey cheese that has been made in Greece since ancient times. 'Xino' literally means sour, but both these cheeses, confusingly, can be either 'sweet' or 'sour'. Served on salads or used in desserts, usually fresh, these are soft and delicious cheeses. There are many cows on Naxos, unlike other islands in the Cyclades, so you can find these cheeses made from cow's milk as well as from sheep's or goat's. Dried Myzithra is sometimes salted and becomes crumbly and hard, stronger in flavour, and a different thing altogether; it can even be grated over pasta. Xinomyzithra is very low in fat, and regarded as a very healthy option.

MASTIC, TURPENTINE AND PISTACHIO

At the end of *A Greek Feast on Naxos*, the guests are given a final drink of mastiha to round off the evening. Mastiha is a clear liqueur often enjoyed as a digestif; it is flavoured with the resin of the mastic tree, and is traditionally made on the Greek island of Chios. As well as being delicious, mastiha has a rather interesting story.

The mastic tree is a low, dense, spreading shrub which, in an unassuming way, is quite beautiful. It grows across the Eastern Mediterranean, enjoying those conditions so familiar in the Cyclades - maquis scrub, oak woodland, rocky hillsides and coastal areas. Its botanic name is *Pistacia lentiscus*, as it is a relative of the tree which gives us pistachio nuts (*Pistacia vera*). In the same family, moreover, is the tree from which we get turpentine (*Pistacia terebinthus*). If you fancy being deeply confused, look into another relative, the *Pistacia atlantica*.

When the resin escapes from the mastic tree (*Pistacia lentiscus*), which happens naturally, it hardens into droplets which, when chewed, have a pleasant, aromatic flavour not unlike chewing gum or pine. You can imagine how this naturally-occurring delicacy was first discovered, can't you? Naturally, there are many stories concerning these so-called 'tears', including that the shrub cried out of pity for Saint Isidorus, whose body was cast beneath it. Such legends are a distraction, however, as are the claims for its health properties, ancient though they are. This is a unique and curious taste. Mastic is used to flavour culinary creations such as cake and ice cream, but it is the liqueur that keeps creeping into *The Naxos Mysteries*. In this form, it bears little resemblance to either pistachios or turpentine …

In the summer of 2012, terrible fires swept across Chios island, destroying more than half the island's mastic trees and more than half the beehives. Nine villages were evacuated and 350 firefighters fought the blaze with water-dropping planes and helicopters. Over the next three days, the whole of Greece suffered from ravaging wildfires. It was sobering to discover recently that the night before the fires on Chios broke out, I had arrived in Athens to begin many weeks travelling round the historical sites of Greece. I wrote this in my diary:

I excused myself from dinner at eleven o'clock. The August night outside was indescribably wonderful: warm, and still not quite dark. The cicadas were particularly loud. Tangible, Greek-scented heat.

KITRON: THE LIQUEUR OF NAXOS
Vallindras Kitron of Naxos

Citron fruit resembles a large lemon in appearance, but is recognisably different in having a lot more pith than soft fruit, a rough rind, and a sharp flavour. Thought to be the 'Median Apple', or 'Persian Apple', mentioned by Theophrastus, it may have begun to arrive in the Mediterranean in the 4th century BCE. Some say it was a symbol of fertility and happiness, appropriately enough for the island of Naxos.

In 1896, Marcos Vallindras, founder of the **Vallindras Distillery in Halki**, produced a unique extract from the leaves of the citron tree (*Citron medica*, meaning citrus of the Medes) and called it 'Kitron of Naxos'. The recipe was preserved and passed down from generation to generation; the fourth and fifth generations of the family run the Kitron distillery today. For more than a century the family have used the original bronze still. You can visit the museum in Halki, learn about the history of the liqueur, and even buy a bottle or two.

Photo: Yiota Vouzna

Vallindras Kitron of Naxos holds a distinguished place among liqueurs, with Protected Designation of Origin (PDO) status in Greece. Its strong scent and flavour come from the highly aromatic essential oils found in the leaves of the citron tree. Kitron is made in three strengths: the yellow has 36% alcohol and very little sugar; the clear has 33% alcohol; and the green has 30% and a distinctive sweetness. It is best served cool in a tulip-shaped glass, which brings out the pleasant taste and aftertaste. As Day and Helen find out, Kitron also makes a delicious cocktail.

GOUNA: SUN-DRIED MACKEREL

I think this is primarily a speciality of Paros, and have certainly seen the shiny brown mackerel hanging out to dry in the sun at a fish taverna on Antiparos, overlooking the smaller island of Despotiko. On Naxos, especially along the main shore road where the tavernas cater for the visitors to the island, these shrivelled-looking fishy treats quickly disappear from the restaurants' displays to be served to those who enjoy their flavour.

Gouna is a traditional way to preserve fish, which is washed, cleaned, and split open with a sharp knife from head to tail down the backbone, leaving the two sides connected in the middle. After being salted and sprinkled with oregano, the gouna are either hung up or laid flat in the hot sun to dry. Several hours later they are ready to be cooked quickly in a hot pan, or on a barbecue or grill, until crisp and well-cooked on the outside but juicy inside. Mackerel are the best for this method of cooking because they are such an 'oily' fish, but other plentiful and 'cheap' fish are also prepared in this way. Gouna are served simply, with a wedge of lemon and a little light salad, crusty bread and a glass of wine.

CAPERS AND CHICKPEAS

Both capers and chickpeas feature prominently in Cycladic cuisine, and while chickpeas are a speciality of Sifnos island, where the chickpea soup called *revithada* must be added to your bucket list, and capers are associated with Tinos, in my mind both form part of the generous cuisine of Naxos. In the recipes in this book, capers appear on salads and chickpeas are prepared as fried vegetable balls.

However, my personal favourite of the two is the caper, still botanically known by its ancient Greek name, *Capparis* (*kappari* in Greek). It's a plant with a mind of its own. It grows like a weed in stone walls, the crevices of old houses, and along the side of the road. It has innocent-looking round leaves that turn to the sun like so many small faces, and beautiful flowers. But beware. It is said that some enterprising islanders (somewhere in the Aegean, if we believe the tale) have attempted to grow it commercially. This was unacceptable to the caper plants, and they failed to thrive. Only the poorest 'soil' would do for them. Consequently the buds must be gathered wherever they can be found, on hands and knees if necessary, towards the end of May and onwards. After a month of soaking, first in water then salt and vinegar, they may be ready to eat. Like many things that demand effort, however, they are worth it (and the flowers *are* beautiful).

Capers *are* grown commercially elsewhere in the Mediterranean region.

OREGANO, SWEET PELARGONIUM AND OTHER HERBS

I was unaware until recently that the Oregano we buy in England is a different plant to the one we eat in Greece. There are about thirty species of oregano, some ten of which grow in Greece. I think that to buy a true Greek oregano plant in the UK you should locate one called *Origanum vulgare subsp. hitrum 'Greek'*. Better still, buy some dried *rigani* on your visit to Naxos and bring it home. Bring some for your friends, too. There seems to be no end to the medicinal properties of Greek oregano, and on the island of Amorgos, near to Naxos, the streets are strewn with *rigani* and sage at Easter, so that as the people walk to church on Good Friday, a wonderful aroma is released. For our purposes, the flavour is even more important. *Rigani* plays a starring role in Greek cuisine, whether meat, fish or vegetable, pasta or eggs or soup.

Sweet Pelargonium, known locally in Greece as *arbaroriza*, is simply the scented-leaved pelargonium often kept in the UK as a houseplant because it is too tender to over-winter here. (It is important that you check that you have bought the right one. Make sure your supplier provides an edible pelargonium.) It is a herb that grows well in the Mediterranean, seeding itself easily and throwing out new roots and shoots. The cooks of Greece use it for flavouring jams, tarts and spoon sweets. The flavour goes particularly well with quinces and grapes. Now you know.

Greek Basil, again, is a different plant from the Italian variety with which we are familiar in the UK. It has smaller leaves and a gentler flavour. Its name is *Ocimum basilicum* (so far like its big Italian cousin), *var. minimum*. Small variety. Greek ladies are frequently to be seen running their hand over the rounded surface of the plant to release the aroma, and some use it when preparing their meatballs, as well as in sauces, salads and fish dishes. You can grow it from seed, and it looks wonderful, but needs watering often.

Mint. I have often worried about mint. Some Greek recipes call for 'mint', others for 'spearmint', and to try to find out whether, in fact, they are interchangeable, I sought out a Greek book called *Green Plants and Herbs of Greece*. It's an interesting book, and according to the authors Garden Mint (*Mentha spicata*) is used in Greece for just about everything; there is no mention of Spearmint. I turned to the Royal Horticultural Society next, who informed me very clearly that they are one and the same plant: *Mentha spicata*. I am reassured. Peppermint, however, was known in Ancient Greece to the Mycenaeans. According to writings on tablets dating from the Bronze Age (1450-1200 BCE), the Mycenaeans were using it to make perfume even then. And we think we are sophisticated (another Greek word).

HONEY

Known as *meli* in Greek (we use the word *mellifluous*, literally meaning flowing honey), Greek honey is one of the most prized in the world. Thyme Honey from the Mount Hymettos area of Athens is best-known, but a small quantity of delicious thyme honey is also made on Iraklia, the small island off Naxos's south coast that appears in *The Disappearance of Ophelia Blue*, and on Naxos itself. Thyme is another of the very important herbs used in Greek cuisine; it likes poor soil, and becomes richer and more fragrant the more sunshine it gets. Look for the blue-painted beehives high on slopes in central Naxos, as seen from the balcony of Day's house in Filoti.

There is growing archaeological interest in whether beekeeping was practised in Prehistoric Greece. Traces of beeswax have been founds on sherds of pots dating from the Greek Middle Neolithic Period (an astonishing 5500 BCE), so honey was known at that time, but evidence of domestic beekeeping is scarce. Only a handful of ceramic smoking pots have been brought to light, and these could have been used for gathering honey from the countryside. However, one of the symbols in the ancient Linear B language, the one which has been deciphered, seems to resemble a horizontal beehive similar to the style of hive used much later in Greece when beekeeping was prevalent. Several early signet rings, too, seem to show beehives of this kind, and men capturing swarming bees.

More relevant to the Greek Foodie, however, is why Greek honey is especially tasty. Some say that it is more dense, and richer in aromatic substances. There are claims that the intensely hot, dry summers intensify the richness of the plants on which the bees gather nectar. Greek honey is also 'raw', meaning non-pasteurised and non-filtered (unlike honeys that are produced to have a longer shelf life). Whatever the reason, a bowl of Greek yogurt topped with Greek honey is supremely delicious, and provides ample calcium, probiotics and *kefi* (zest for life).

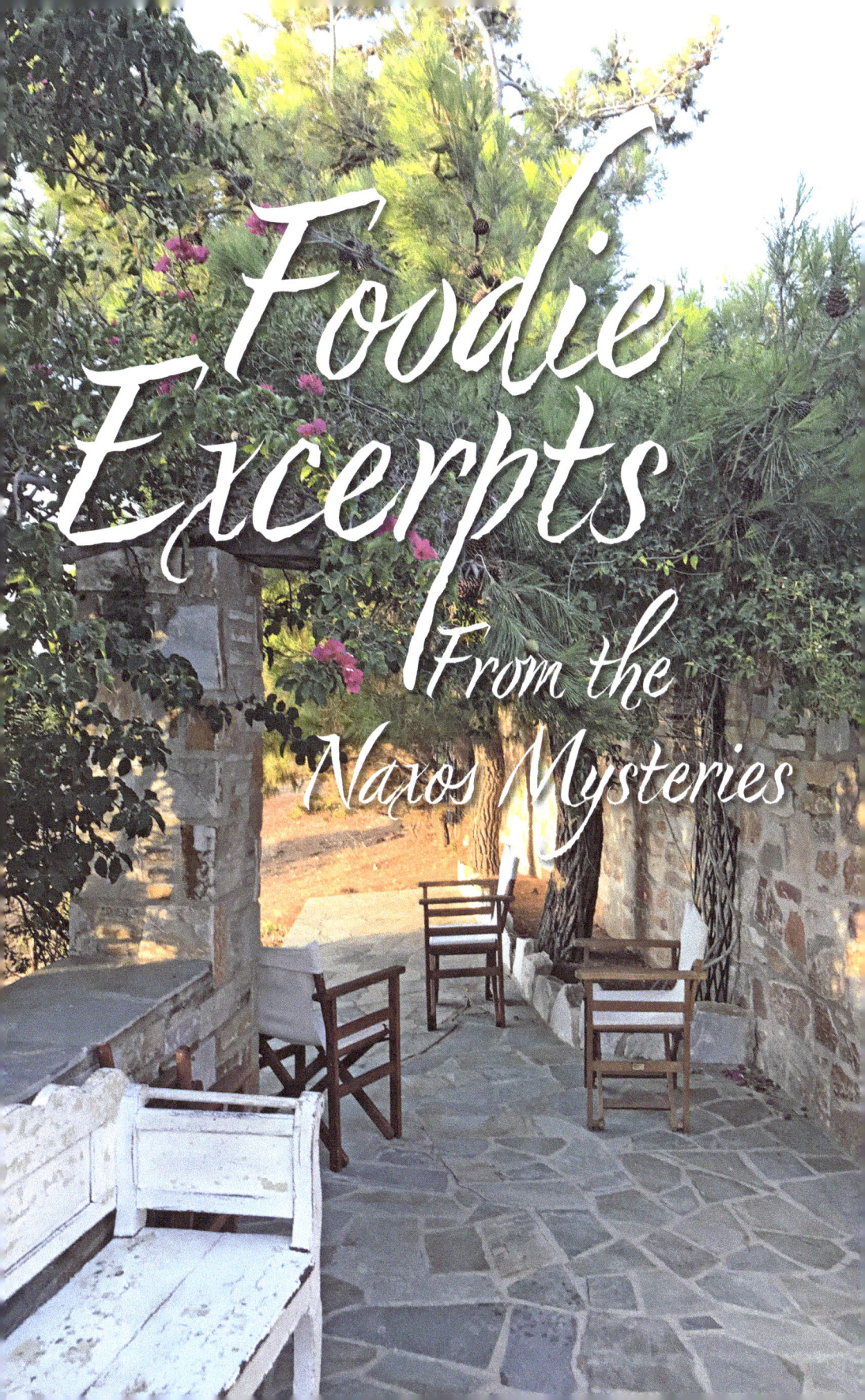

FOODIE EXCERPTS FROM
THE NAXOS MYSTERIES

Day soon felt decidedly light-headed. The wine was delicious, cool and scented as with an aroma of mountain herbs, and Aristos was generous with it. He and Aristos shared a love of wine, just as they shared a love of Greece, of archaeology, of beauty, and of peacefulness.

They ate Rania's delicately seasoned stew of lamb and potatoes with satisfaction. The lamb fell off the bone, the sauce was subtly flavoured with local oregano, and the chunks of local potatoes were rich with the flavour of the meat. Day thought Rania's cooking exemplified the best of Greek cuisine and never turned down an invitation to eat her food. There were the usual extras, too: an olive-rich Greek salad boasting large chunks of tasty tomato and juicy onion, and extra homemade fried potatoes especially for Day, who had a rather soft spot for chips.

There was fresh fruit to follow. Day politely declined the fruit, as usual. Dessert wasn't his thing, he would say. Oddly, this applied to fruit, which he didn't object to but rarely ate. He helped himself to seconds of chips when he thought nobody would notice.

The Meaning of Friday

They started on the food with enthusiasm. The small plates of appetisers were delicate, and the bread fresh. The thin slices of aubergine had been lightly dusted with fine batter which had crisped in the frying. The village sausage was served in dainty pieces and wallowed in a sauce rich with tomato. Best of all was the *fava*, yellow split pea dip, slightly warm and topped with a splash of green olive oil and crunchy bits of finely chopped onion.

They ordered a portion of cockerel, a Greek salad and some fries. Thanasis persuaded them that instead of fries they should try his wife's home-style fried potatoes, which were slices of the waxy local potatoes perfectly crisped in the oven and topped with oregano and olive oil.

They shared all the dishes between them and Day admitted that the home-fried potato slices were superb, even for a lover of chips such as himself. The potatoes on Naxos had a well-deserved reputation for excellence. He raised his glass to her with a sense of theatre.

'Here's to a wonderful, productive summer in the Cyclades. A great new novel for you, the biography of a generation for me, and a great deal of down-time and good food.'

'To the summer.'

Day waved the empty wine jug in Thanasis's direction and caught his eye.

'Thanasi, another jug, please, just a small one.'

The Meaning of Friday

They walked as usual to the taverna. It was dark, the cool breeze had disappeared, and it was warmer than a few hours earlier. Helen loved this about Greece, the dark warmth of the night, eating late.

Thanasis's son, Vangelis, was on duty in the restaurant and introduced himself. Thanasis then arrived at their table with a half litre of white wine in a chilled metal jug, before Day and Helen had even ordered.

'This is on the house,' said Thanasis. 'It's a white wine made by my family in their own small vineyard. I'd like you to try it, and I'll bring you some small dishes to have with it.'

The small dishes were more generous than Helen and Day expected. There was aubergine dip, vinegary 'politiki' salad and delicate pieces of boiled octopus in lemon juice. All talk of the Moralis question was postponed as they ate and drank. The wine was dry but quite tasty, and the sharp little salad and fresh fishy bites complemented it well.

Day used a piece of bread to finish the aubergine dip.

'Very kind of Thanasis. To be honest, though, I could murder a plate of chips and a glass of red,' he said in a low voice.

The Meaning of Friday

She was interrupted by a smiling Thanasis, apologising for not coming to welcome them before. He put two clean plates in front of them, asked to know if they were well, commented on the weather, and expressed his pleasure that they had ordered his wife's souvlaki.

He was followed by Vangelis, carrying a dish in each hand and one balanced on his forearm. He placed the chips before Day with a rather knowing smile. A local salad that shone with freshness and olive oil was set down by Helen, and next to it a homemade tzatziki, the tasty yogurt and mint dip traditionally served with souvlaki.

The door to the kitchen opened, and Thanasis's wife brought over her speciality. It gave off an aroma that made their tastebuds tingle. There was much thanking and smiling and nodding before she returned to her domain to produce another miracle.

The Meaning of Friday

'What is horta?' asked the Sicilian.

'It's just very simple steamed green leaves, grown locally, probably picked today. There are a number of different leaves they use, but they're all delicious. The octopus should be excellent, good choice. We don't really need a filler, but the potatoes on Naxos are renowned for their flavour; the locals are extremely proud of them. You have to have them at your first meal here.'

Thus Day concealed his love of Naxian chips beneath a veneer of hospitality.

The Search for Artemis

The old wooden table in the main room of Day's house now bore a magnificent centrepiece - a large old plate which Day had found in the larder when he moved into the house. On it lay a fish, a Mediterranean sea bass called a lavraki in Greece, grilled and dressed with oil, garlic, chilli, lemon and thyme. In another dish were shrimps in a tomato sauce with a little melted Feta cheese. A bowl of rocket, one of Day's favourite things, flanked a dish of traditional Greek salad or horiatiki. Everyone began with the shrimp dish, eating it with bread: Helen had found a suitable bread basket in one of Day's cupboards. She then slit the skin of the fish with a practised hand, eased the flesh from the bones, and invited everyone to help themselves.

'I thought we could have cheese on the balcony,' she suggested when they were finished. She had prepared a platter of cheeses, including not only local Mizithra but a piece of Long Clawson Stilton which she had smuggled out from London in her suitcase and which had miraculously survived the journey. Soon they were sitting with their plates and small glasses of red wine on the balcony, just in time for that precious moment of evening when the sun, having vanished behind the opposite hills but not below the distant horizon, attracted attention to itself with pulsations of amber and gold.

The Search for Artemis

The young waiter grinned.

'We have octopus and shrimp, fresh today. I highly recommend them. We also have mussels cooked in my mother's own sauce. For meat, we have lamb chops grilled, and rooster in red sauce. The special salad today is "politiki" salad. The shrimps we can grill, fry or cook "saganaki": that's with Feta cheese. The octopus grilled, or with lemon sauce, or my favourite way, which is with macaroni in a tomato sauce. It's a dish we usually eat in Lent, but it's very popular, so we offer it at other times of the year, too.'

The Search for Artemis

He went to find Helen, who was taking a break from work to prepare something to eat. They took their usual light lunch to the balcony table; it consisted of cheese, rocket, olives and grilled flatbread moistened with thick local olive oil. It was another hot August day, and they drank most of a bottle of cold mineral water.

'We'll need to visit the supermarket in Chora soon,' observed Day. 'I've run out of lemons.'

'That will never do. What will you put in your gin and tonic?'

Although lemons were absolutely essential for Day's signature gin and tonic, which he had turned into an art form, Helen had noticed that the stock of food in Day's kitchen was very low. Day was less than enthusiastic about most fruit, and only knew vegetables when they were brought to him in a restaurant.

'Now, what does your clever wife have in the kitchen today?' he asked.

Thanasis knew what he meant: the dishes of the day made with fresh produce that inspired his wife Koula to feats of culinary genius.

'Today she has some excellent veal,' he began, turning up his face as he spoke as if to enjoy the warmth of the sun. 'So, there is grilled veal chop, or a tasty veal with eggplant - or aubergine, as I think the British call it. Or there is a veal *kelaidi*.'

Day and Helen exchanged a glance, but clearly neither had heard of this before.

'*Kelaidi* is a dish from Northern Greece, near Larissa. My wife's sister lives there and gave her this recipe. A small heap of tender veal shoulder is placed in a dish and topped with layers of onion, tomato and green pepper. It is cooked slowly, then topped with Feta or Kefalotyri cheese, which is allowed to melt over the Kelaidi in the oven.' He lowered his voice. 'The secret ingredients are melted butter and a lot of garlic!'

Since there was clearly no possibility of choosing anything else, Helen asked what Thanasis recommended to accompany the *kelaidi*.

'Ah, La Belle Helene!' he beamed. 'For you and Martin I propose the *patates fournou* - our finest Naxian potatoes roasted with olive oil and oregano - and then something simple and clean for the palate, such as a salad of cabbage and carrot. You know this? It is raw sliced vegetables softened in salted water, rinsed well, and dressed with oil and lemon juice. Delicious, and very healthy!'

Despite the substitution of roast potatoes for his beloved chips, Day had to agree that this was a meal worthy of the occasion. With a small bow and another smile at Helen, Thanasis departed for the kitchen.

He returned within minutes carrying a tray. He placed a small bottle of ouzo, a jug of cold water and a bowl of ice cubes on the table, and added a small dish divided into three which held olives, slices of sweet pepper and delicate cubes of hard cheese.

'The food will be a little while, my friends, so please enjoy a little ouzo on the house while you're waiting.'

Day brought the tray closer to him, placed a chunk of ice in each glass and added a measure of the clear distilled liquid. The ouzo began to turn cloudy on contact with the ice. He handed one to Helen, who added a little water. The aroma of aniseed brought a smile to their faces.

'Cheers.'

'*Stin yia sas*!'

Black Acorns

A tantalising platter of cold meats and cheeses, most of which were new and intriguing, was put before them. The veal with mushrooms and *trahana* arrived shortly afterwards, followed by a house salad with walnuts and crumbled Feta cheese. Day poured a glass of water for Helen and then for himself, and refilled their wine glasses, which as usual were tiny. They ate contentedly until the dishes were practically empty.

'I wonder what Greek cuisine would look like if there was no cheese,' mused Day.

'Impossible to even guess,' said Helen.

Black Acorns

Back in the kitchen he surveyed the mound of remaining ingredients and began to chop. Unsure of quantities, he erred on the generous side. As he peeled the onions and cut them into chunks, he reflected that it looked rather a lot. He washed the green peppers, removed the insides and chopped these too before throwing them, with the onion, into the largest baking pan he could find in the oven drawer. This reminded him to put the oven on to warm up.

He had a sudden qualm that the dish would not be flavoursome enough. Pulling out a clean bowl, he spooned in some chilli flakes, salt, pepper and more sumac, and mixed them all together. With his hands he extracted the chicken from the marinade a fillet at a time, and rubbed some spice mixture into each sticky piece with his hands, putting the finished chunks of meat on top of his vegetables. To Day it looked extremely impressive, and he had a little private smile. Now he was left with some dry spices and some marinade. I'll mix them and add them to the pan, he thought, and did so. He poured over a generous quantity of red wine and some hot water from the kettle, and put the pan in the oven.

(*Some time later*)

The Middle Eastern Chicken was looking good, so he loosened the roast potatoes that had stuck to the pan and put it back into the oven while he made the salad.

A Celebration of Cuisine in the Cyclades from the author of The Naxos Mysteries

That done, he carried the plates and cutlery to the balcony and set them out on the table. He saw Helen looking at him over Rania's shoulder and winked at her. She returned the wink.

The last thing to do was open the bottle of wine he had chosen to go with his meal. That done, he carried first the tray of chicken, then the salad, and finally the wine and a bottle of water to the balcony table.

There was enough to feed everyone for several days.

Black Acorns

'What would you like to eat?' Helen asked, taking a discreet look at the food on the other tables before studying the menu. 'How about a selection of small *orektika* tonight?'

Day readily agreed; *orektika*, or appetisers, were a very good way to taste as many delicious things as possible in Greece.

'You can choose whatever you fancy for us, as long as you order me some chips.'

'Naturally,' she said, and shot a smile at the waiter which had him instantly at their side. After a polite exchange of banter, during which Helen could feel the fluency of her Greek returning satisfactorily, the waiter raised his pencil slightly above his notebook and asked what they would like to drink.

Having already scanned the wine menu, Day asked for a bottle of Xinomavro red wine. It was not the cheapest bottle on the list, but it felt like a particularly special night. He had a strange sense of impending success.

'And to eat?' asked the waiter, enjoying himself.

'Some dishes to share, please,' said Helen. 'We'll have a Feta *ravasaki*, some of the zucchini balls, the grilled Anavra sausages, fried calamari and a rocket salad. Oh, and a portion of fried potatoes. Thank you.'

The man bowed and turned away, clicking his fingers towards a younger waiter and lifting his chin imperiously. He passed the food order to him and almost ran down the stairs leading to the ground floor, returning with the expensive bottle of Xinomavro, which he twisted in front of Day.

When the wine was in their glasses, most of the food on the table and the chips at his right hand, Day was extremely happy. He raised his glass in a toast.

'To another wonderful evening in Greece,' he said.

The Disappearance of Ophelia Blue

No sooner had they sat down than they were invited to the kitchen to choose their food. Three women were busy among the stainless steel surfaces, gleaming gas hobs and deep ovens. It was a surprisingly modern scene in contrast to the traditional house. Fresh fish and seafood were displayed on ice in a glass-fronted cabinet, and the hot food was steaming in vast aluminium trays. There was a gently bubbling pan of artichokes in some tempting sauce, roasted chicken legs on a bed of *manestra*, aubergines cooked with tomatoes and cheese, and a tray of beef and potatoes topped with fresh green herbs. More dishes seemed to be still cooking. The owner pointed out the array of salads and reminded them of the ways in which any of the fresh fish could be prepared, then looked at them expectantly for their answer.

'*Perimenetay!*' called the oldest woman, waving at her husband and uncovering another tray of food that she had just brought out of an oven. When the fragrant steam dispersed, they saw fine strands of spaghetti topped with mussels and cockles in their shells and generous pieces of lobster.

The Disappearance of Ophelia Blue

After consulting the menu, they ordered a gilt-head bream, called tsipoura in Greek, for the highlight of the meal. It would be baked in parchment with olive oil, lemon and oregano. While the tsipoura was being cooked, they started with a small plate of tender baby squid, the rings and frond-like pieces of tentacle dusted in flour and fried to perfection. With this came the yellow split pea dip called fava, served slightly warm with a sprinkling of chopped onion and a drizzle of olive oil, to be scooped up with bread. The last little side-dish was a Greek potato salad made with the fine produce of Naxos dressed with chopped spring onions, olive oil and fresh herbs.

Over at the courtyard entrance, the young waiter stood waiting, and on hearing his name he crossed the lane to the restaurant's kitchen and returned with a large platter. He brought it to their table and opened the parchment to reveal the *tsipoura*, fragrant with lemon, herbs and a warm smell of the sea.

'*Kali orexi!*' he announced, and left them to enjoy their meal. Helen drew a knife gently down the central bone of the fish and pushed away the skin. The white flesh of the bream came away from the bones easily, releasing fragrant steam.

'Now this really is Greek cuisine at its best - simple and fresh,' said Helen.

The Disappearance of Ophelia Blue

The table was cleared and Rania went inside to fetch the main course, roasted Greek lamb with potatoes. Fragrant with herbs and garlic, the aroma of the meat was rich with lemon juice and white wine, and the potatoes had been cooked in the tray with the joint. They had absorbed the meat juice and were full of its flavour, but their tops remained crisp. Nestoras was the only person at the table who noticed Day, who loved potatoes in any form, quietly helping himself to one or two more.

The lamb course was followed by a dessert. Deppi had made a *myzithropita,* the nearest thing in Greece to a cheesecake and a traditional recipe from the nearby island of Syros, where she grew up. It was a rich combination of the soft local cheese,

honey, cinnamon and grated orange peel. Nestoras had a large portion and a second helping. Day was almost sorry that he had no liking for sweet food.
The Disappearance of Ophelia Blue

The supermarket was on the outskirts of Chora, just off the road from Filoti. There were already quite a few cars on the gravelled parking area, and fresh produce was still being unloaded from vans and stacked by the front door. A local hotelier was intercepting what he needed before it could even be laid out. Day and Helen had a system for food shopping. Helen would pick up the meat, salad and what Day called 'cooking stuff', while he shopped for snacks and drinks. First, he put a six-pack of mineral water into his trolley, not because there was anything wrong with the local water, but because it was easier to chill it in the fridge. As Helen went to the meat counter and began to ask for what she wanted, Day walked directly to examine the wine, where he quickly became absorbed.

'Right,' he said when they met up again, 'I have water, drinks, nibbles, lemons and that kind of thing. What else do you want me to get?'

'Coffee? Bread? I suppose it's no use giving you the job of fruit or vegetables, is it? I'll do that, and I'll meet you at the till. Oh, you get the olive oil, too.'

Day nodded; he loved a really good olive oil, mopped up with fresh bread or drizzled over rocket. He studied the shelves carefully, finally choosing a small tin of Cretan Extra Virgin, which he hoped would be full of flavour and that tempting green colour that he associated with certain good oils. A packet of coffee and two bags of the delicious local flatbreads completed his task.

He looked with interest at the contents of Helen's trolley as they waited at the till. There were packs of meat, hand-wrapped and labelled, and similar parcels from the cheese counter. He approved of the bunch of fresh rocket and the bag of dark red tomatoes, but he could never really understand why she bought so much fruit.
The Disappearance of Ophelia Blue

A generous portion of the *trahanas*-stuffed vegetables had been carefully arranged on a deep plate, which Thanasis placed before them with pride. He returned with a dish of tiny, tender lamb chops grilled to perfection, and the essential chips, which he put within easy reach of Day with a smile.

'If you could eat nothing else on Naxos,' he said, indicating the stuffed vegetables, 'this dish would give you the essence of Greek home cooking. *Kali orexi*!'

He walked away to welcome some newly-arrived guests and offer them a table. Day took a little of the *yemista*, enjoying the aroma of baked cheese and savoury juices that arose from it. The crunchy, dark brown lids of the baked tomatoes, which had been topped with breadcrumbs and olive oil before being cooked in the oven, gave way with a pleasing amount of resistance to his fork. He took a first mouthful.

'Oh, that's good. You know me, Helen, not a huge fan of vegetables, but I might just be converted by this. I like the *trahanas* as a change from rice. More wine?' He poured a little more of the 'barrel' wine into their small glasses, helped himself to a couple of the delicate lamb chops and, finally, took a portion of chips.

The Disappearance of Ophelia Blue

He was debating whether to have any wine, a debate which he rarely held with himself, when Vangelis arrived with a jug of it. The debate had been concluded. Vangelis also brought a small *horiatiki* salad which Day had not ordered but which someone in the kitchen had apparently decided he needed. The crisp cucumber, tasty tomatoes and local white cheese, to which he added a generous application of olive oil, served only to increase his appetite for the meal. Even the onions that lay scattered in fine slices across the salad were mild and juicy, and he ate each piece with a little of the fresh bread. He left only the olives, to which he was not partial. When he had finished everything else, he put down his fork and sat back, glass in hand.

The main course arrived sooner than expected. The *giouvetsi* looked and smelled excellent; just the comfort food he needed. The small shank of tender lamb, traditionally cooked for a long time in the clay giouvetsi pot, rested on a bed of *kritharaki*, the rice-shaped pasta known in Italy as orzo. It was all softly wallowing in a light sauce of ripe tomatoes, garlic and a touch of lemon. The fact that he had no need of the additional chips would make no difference to his enjoyment of them, and it was with them that he started.

The Reach of the Past

Day went to the kitchen and opened the fridge. When he had said there was food, he had been rather over-confident. There was plenty to eat for himself alone, because he would have been content with a plate of left-overs, but now he would have to be creative. He had potatoes, so he would roast a lot of them. There were plenty of tomatoes, a cucumber and an onion, and he had oregano, olive oil, and black pepper. He was already happy with that; a salad would be easy. What else?

There was no meat. A bag of dried split peas caught his eye. Could he make a *fava*, Helen's favourite? He had once watched her make one using a recipe from an old Greek cookbook they had found in the house. He decided to give it a try.

He reckoned Fabrizio would be there within the hour, but that gave him enough time to get the food going. He peeled and cut far too many potatoes and put them in a baking tray with plenty of good Greek oil, lemon juice squeezed from one of his precious lemons, oregano and salt. He switched on the oven and put the potatoes in to cook.

Now for the *fava*, having found the old recipe. Rinse the split peas, boil water, cook for half an hour. Grate an onion, cook it, add to the split peas, season… With luck, they would have a meal of sorts. He could make the salad later. At least there was no shortage of drink in the house.

The Reach of the Past

She suggested a Cretan restaurant not far from the museum, a place she went to often and could recommend. She reminded him that she did not eat meat or fish, and he shrugged.

'Great. You can order for both of us.'

A glance at the menu told him the place was inexpensive, and the portions were generous when they came. Efi ordered Cretan *dakos*, the rusk that resembled a bruschetta, topped with tomato and a crumbled Cretan cheese; a *boureki*, which was a gratin made from courgettes, potatoes and cheese; a salad with cold potato, tomatoes, boiled egg and something called *kritamo*; and little *hortopites*, which were miniature pies containing wild greens and herbs.

'And we must have the fries,' she said. 'They're really good here. They come with a special sauce.'

Day watched the arrival of the food with pleasure, realising how hungry he was. They drank water and ate with relish. The *kritamo*, which Day had never tried before, turned out to be like samphire, a branched and shiny wild plant from the coasts of Crete. Efi informed him that its health properties had been well known since the time of the Ancient Greeks. It was not unpleasant, reminding him of seaweed. She regaled him with a list of the vitamins in the plant, and told him it provided quantities of omega 3, iodine, and antioxidants. The list went on and on.

'They say it's good for the libido also,' she concluded with a chuckle.

'I'm just happy that it's good for the liver,' murmured Day, recalling his evening with Fabrizio and helping himself to the chips.

The Reach of the Past

When Thanasis had seated his latest arrivals, a large group of tourists from Chora, they had a chance to ask him what was cooking in the kitchen.

'We have veal with artichokes, sea bream, and *paidakia*. I remember the little chops are one of your favourites, Martin. Also, in honour of the concert tonight, there is a shrimp *saganaki* made with a very special Naxian cheese.'

He bent down to them and almost whispered in his enthusiasm.

'I recommend that you begin with a small portion of this cheese, perhaps with a few other little *mezedes* and another ouzo. My good friend Dimitris is the cheese-maker. He is renowned on Naxos and his cheeses are highly admired throughout the Cyclades. We sometimes call this one "black cheese" because of the dark colour of the outside … what is the English word?'

'Rind.'

'That's it. This cheese is yellow and salty and delicious! I find it slightly spicy. Excellent for cooking, but also quite delicious to eat on its own.'

He leaned in slightly towards Day.

'Its name, Arseniko, means "male", Martin. So it must be good for us men, no?'

The Reach of the Past

They arrived back at the table just in time for the first course. The mussels were steaming with a fragrant aroma of ouzo, the delicate pieces of raw tuna were softened and cured in a light dressing of the local citrus liqueur, and Fotini's salad was piquant with bitter chicory and the pungent sweet-and-sour Xinotyro cheese.

The main dishes were no less delicious than the first course. Day and Andreas were unable to think when they had eaten better steak, and Day was gratified when the food arrived with a side portion of fried potatoes. He caught an amused glance from Helen, who was expertly opening her prawns in a far more delicate manner than he had ever managed. The most beautiful dish, however, was Fotini's. The fillet of *tsipoura* with its piquant sauce and orange-scented couscous looked like something from a Michelin-starred restaurant.

The Reach of the Past

A DRIVE ROUND NAXOS ISLAND
with *The Naxos Mysteries*

Begin at the bus terminal at Chora, near the approach to the Portara. Take a bus or taxi to Agios Prokopios, where you will readily see a good place to hire a car. Negotiate good terms for several days - you'll thank me later.

From Agios Prokopios, where you will already (of course) have taken a walk and recognised that this is a place dripping with tavernas and have decided to come back after this adventure, head towards Agia Anna on the coastal (and only) road. Along the way there are two notable places to which I would like to draw your attention. One is the venue for live music, Art Cafe, which you should investigate. There is a summer-long programme of bouzouki, guitar and classical music, and a number of other excellent things which you might book. Nearby, however, you must park your car and take a cool drink at the little roadside bar belonging to the taverna 'O Fotis'. Consisting of only a handful of tables right next to the sea, this must be one of our favourite little bars on Naxos's south coast, and features on the cover of *The Reach of the Past*. Make a point of returning just before sunset, sitting with the drink of your choice, and watching the sun set gloriously behind Paros, sending golden colours shooting across the water towards you. Agios Prokopios is, by the way, where the boat fire took place in *Black Acorns*.

Drive on to Agia Anna. You already know, of course, that *Agios* means saint, and *Agia* is the feminine form. Agia Anna is a popular tourist village, with particularly nice swimming in the bay to the extreme left as you stand on the beach and look towards the sea. Swim out to the rocks overlooking Paros, where those in the know have also discovered a tiny, quiet beach. Helen swims here in *The Meaning of Friday*. After drying off in the sun, make your way back to the tavernas that front the boardwalk and beach, find yourself a cocktail, or visit a fish taverna. One of these is the taverna featured at the end of *The Meaning of Friday*, where Day and Helen say goodbye to Alex and Kate.

The road continues from Agia Anna to Plaka. Plaka is a very busy beach, long and hot … but high above it is (perhaps only in my imagination) the house which Nick has restored for Deppi and his young family in *The Disappearance of Ophelia Blue*. If you climb up behind the beach you can see the same view. Having done that, back in the car, find the 'cedar forest' at Alyko beach, wander the white sand dunes and see if you can spot the many birds and even hares that are protected in this nature reserve. The lovely Axiotissa Restaurant is on your route home, and will make you very welcome.

ONLINE SUPPLIERS OF GREEK INGREDIENTS AND FOODS IN THE UK

The suppliers below are not aware of the recommendation I am giving in this book, and have certainly not paid to advertise here. I offer this to readers simply because I have tried these suppliers myself, and, on the occasions I have used them, I have been happy with the outcome.

This is not a guarantee of the service or quality you may receive from them yourselves. Please regard this list as a starting point, and may it lead to many happy sessions making and eating Greek food.

Maltby & Greek *www.maltbyandgreek.com*
The Hellenic Deli *www.thehellenicdeli.com*
Hellenic Grocery *www.hellenicgrocery.co.uk*
Oliveology *www.oliveology.co.uk*

A FEW SUGGESTIONS
Further reading for the 'Greek Foodie'

Around the Cooking Pot of 'Axiotissa' **Yiannis Vassilas**
The Foods of the Greek Islands **Aglaia Kremezi**
The Foods of Greece **Aglaia Kremezi**
Cycladic Culture and Gastronomy **Friends of Paros and Antiparos**
The Wines of Greece **Konstantinos Lazarakis**
Green Plants & Herbs of Greece **Vangelis Papiomytoglou** & **Nikos Nikitidis**
Mediterranean Escapes **Rick Stein**
Cycladic Cuisine **Nikoleta Delatola-Foskolou**
My Greek Meze **Eleni Psyhouli** & **Ioanna Pavlaki**
Smashing Plates **Maria Elia**

www.akispetretzikis.com
www.olivetomato.com
www.eatyourselfgreek.com

SOME GREEK EXPLAINED

In the story, as in the *Mysteries*, Greek words and expressions are used for authenticity. Regular readers will be used to this by now, but it's always handy to have the translations nearby. These words are in italics, as are some quite common phrases in French and Italian. Food names are explained in the text and mostly reoccur in the recipes.

Kyries kai Kyrioi! Ladies and Gentlemen!

Na zisete! *Na sas xaireste*!
Both these phrases are used to congratulate the newly-married couple. Literally meaning 'may you live' and 'may you be happy', they both convey a wish that the couple enjoy a long life together full of health and happiness. Both phrases are thought to have originated when there was significant infant mortality, and was addressed to a child as well as to the wedding couple.

Kali orexi! Bon appetit!

Kalo kalokairi Happy (or good) summer, often used as another good wish.

Oriste! Here you are!

Endaxi? All right?

Syrtaki This is the well-known Greek dance made famous in *Zorba the Greek*

INDEX OF RECIPES

'Apollon' salad 33
Arni sto Fourno 42
Aubergines:
    Melitzanosalata 28
    Aubergine and Pomegranate Pâté 29
    Kalogeros 47
Beef:
    Kalogeros 47
    Keftedes 36
    Yemista 44, 45
Beetroot salad 34
Biscuits: Cookies with Orange & Cinnamon 51
Cake: Tou Yiaourtiou 49
Courgettes: Kolokythokeftedes 40
Dips:
    Fava 26
    Melitzanosalata 28
    Tzatziki 35
Domatokeftedes 37, 39
Eggplants, see Aubergines
Eggplant caviar 29
Fava 26
Fennel Fritters 41
'Filarakia' salad 33
Glika tou Koutaliou 52
Horiatiki (Greek) Salad 32

Kalogeros 47
Keftedes 36
Kolokythokeftedes 40
Koulourakia 51
Kremezi, Aglaia, recipes 49, 51
Lamb: Arni Sto Fourno 42
Meatballs: 36
Melitzanosalata 28
Pies: 30, 31
Pitarakia 31
Patates Fournou 43
Potatoes: 43
Salads: 32, 33, 34
Stuffed Vegetables 44, 45
Spoon Sweets 52
Tomatoes:
    Domatokeftedes 37, 39
    Yemista 44, 45
Tou Yiaourtiou 49
Tyropitakia 30
Tzatziki 35
Vassilas, Yiannis, recipes 29, 34, 41, 45
Yellow Split Pea Dip 26
Yemista 44, 45
Zucchini, see Courgettes